PETER PRAN
OF ELLERBE BECKET

Architectural Monographs No 24

PETER PRAN

OF ELLERBE BECKET
RECENT WORKS

A.D. ACADEMY EDITIONS

TO MY WIFE CLEVON PRAN

Architectural Monographs No 24
Editorial Offices
42 Leinster Gardens London W2 3AN

ISSN 0141-2191

Publisher
Dr Andreas C Papadakis

Editorial and Design Team: Andrea Bettella (Senior Designer); Nicola Hodges (Editorial); Jacqueline Grosvenor; Annamarie Uhr

Subscriptions
Mira Joka

Architect's note
I wish to express my deep gratitude to Andreas Papadakis for his initiation of and commitment to this publication of my work. Recognising his continuous, consistent and unsurpassed international leadership in the presentation of the most innovative architecture of our times, I am deeply honoured. My heartfelt thanks are due to three colleagues who have inspired and supported me: Kenneth Frampton, the foremost architecture critic of our times; Fumihiko Maki, one of the few living master architects; and Daniel Libeskind, one of the most brilliant architects and thinkers today. I am honoured by their words. I am also fortunate to have the trust and support of very special clients. Their collaboration has unfailingly enhanced our and my efforts in every instance illustrated here. Ellerbe Becket has afforded me and the other collaborators wonderful opportunities to explore and develop my and the design teams' directions in design within the context of the firm's commitment to creating extraordinary architecture for its clients. I take great pride in the personal contributions we/I have made to the firm's emerging design leadership. And lastly, a special thankyou to each of the outstanding individuals I have worked with or received advice and support from over the years.

Cover: Saudi Corporate Headquarters, Jeddah, 1992, model, photo by Dan Cornish;
page 2: Deloitte & Touche Headquarters, executive area, Wilton, Connecticut, 1989

First published in Great Britain in 1992 by
ACADEMY EDITIONS
An imprint of the Academy Group Ltd
42 Leinster Gardens London W2 3AN
A Member of VCH Publishing Group

ISBN 1 85490 168 0 (HB)
ISBN 1 85490 169 9 (PB)

Published in the United States of America in 1992 by
ST MARTIN'S PRESS
175 Fifth Avenue, New York, NY 10012

ISBN 0-312-08689-X (HB)
ISBN 0-312-08690-3 (PB)

Printed and bound in Singapore

CONTENTS

DANIEL LIBESKIND
A Personal Statement

It is not often that I am asked to provide an introduction to a book which deals with an architect whose work is part of the corporate world. I have followed with interest, however, the architectural work of Peter Pran, since he surely represents the best in the large American architectural firms.

His personal committment to architecture has been to elevate through his energy and his own considerable creative talent the often banal and expedient, to the level of large-scale innovation and the untested.

The contents of this book offer an impressive array of commercial works which attempts to push the limits of corporate architecture and establish a new and potentially exciting realm.

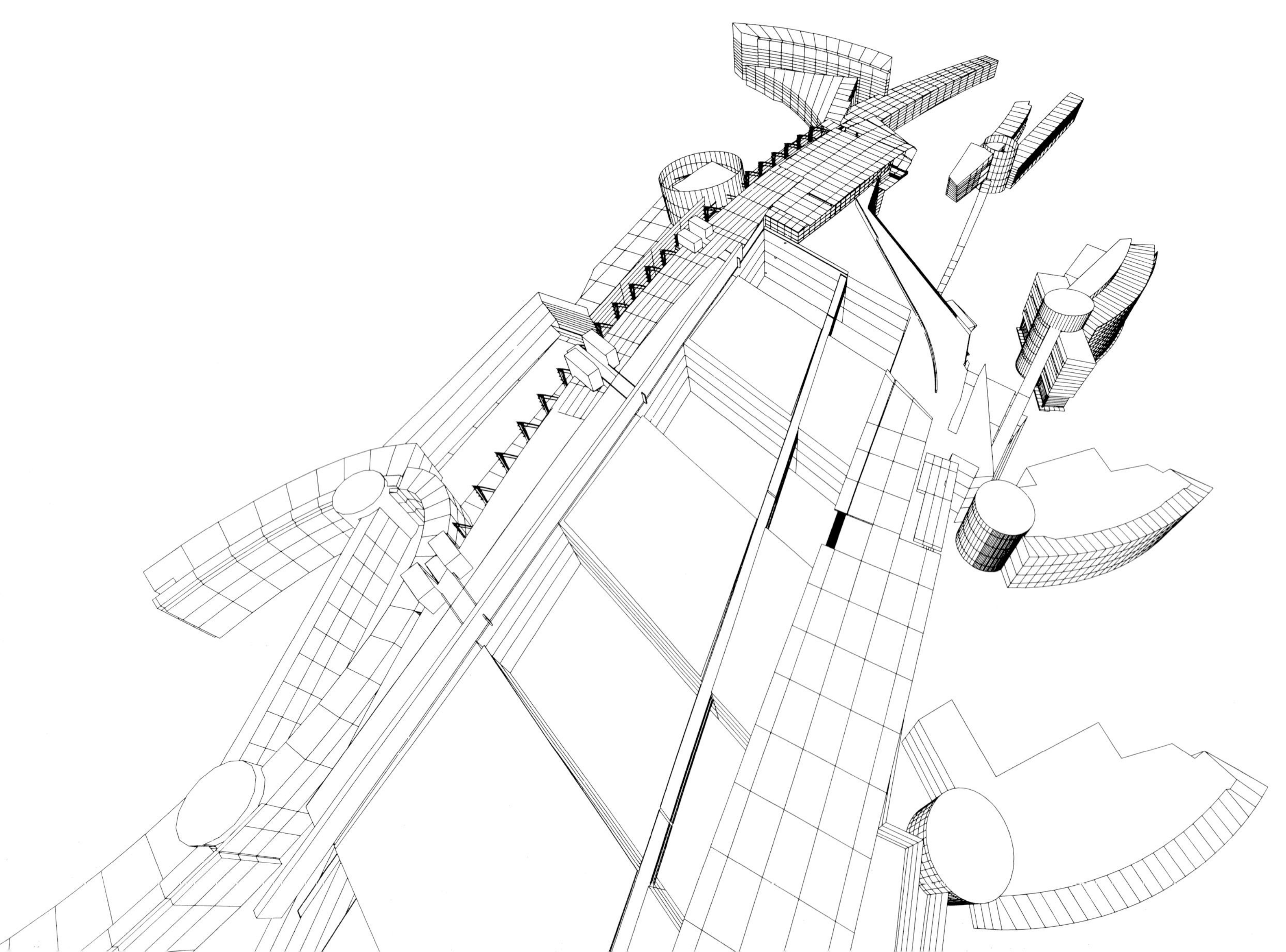

FUMIHIKO MAKI
On Peter Pran

Cubism and De Stijl were perhaps the first artistic movements that recognised the visual complexity of our world; by registering our altered perception of the visible world, those artists gave birth to a new conception of modernity. Today, nearly a century after the emergence of the artistic avant-garde, we still find ourselves in search of modernity, an ideal whose essence lies in the quest of defining what and where we are now. The task shows little sign of exhausting itself, for it is the ever-changing present that modernity claims as its final and supreme flower.

The technological advances and the coming together of cultures during our time have greatly expanded our ability to see, hear, analyse, and communicate the complexity of our world. Our increased awareness of this complexity allows us more than ever to perceive intricate relations between the trivial actions of everyday life and the global issues our society faces. Thus our materialistic desire for higher living standards is now seen in the context of the need to conserve natural resources; our pursuit of larger economic networks, in the context of maintaining smaller ethnic and cultural identities; our aspiration for excellence, in the context of an egalitarian faith in common good for the common man. Modernity thrives on conflict, dilemma, and irony, which continuously challenge our curiosity and capacity to reason.

Within this intellectual climate, it is not difficult to see in each of the myriad artistic works being produced today an intentional response to this notion of complexity. This may be particularly true in the field of architecture, an art whose functional grounding has historically required a high level of synthesis of complex goals. Today the architect is regularly asked to make sense of an ever-increasing list of programmatic requirements and performance expectations, and the creation of good architectural space at times requires a nearly superhuman effort to overcome the trivial and the tangential. Some designers might address the issue of complexity by simple denial; in this sense, the minimalist aesthetic makes a strong commentary on our times. Other designers choose instead to take advantage of the very energy of complexity; for them, the overlapping, contradictory conditions of our times provoke a saturated visual response based on sensual collage.

The work of Peter Pran belongs to this second school – the School of Complexity – in fact, he might be called one of the School's foremost advocates. Pran's design builds on a fragmentary aesthetic of floating planar elements that seem to deny gravity and blur distinctions between inside and outside space; in this, he makes use of the legacy of De Stijl compositional principles. Yet his formal vocabulary is far richer than the sober orthogonal world of those earlier Dutch modernists; in particular, his use of curved surfaces in close juxtaposition to orthogonal lines to create considerable tension within and between spaces. The contrast of straight and curved lines, rather than merely the curve itself, is responsible for the richness of visual and spatial experience in his projects. The sensual abandon with which Pran shapes spaces of passage and points of juncture lends the entire spatial composition a strong sense of fluidity and movement. Yet there is a high degree of control, precision, and logic that determines these curves in the end; one never senses that his architecture has left the realm of rational constructs.

Pran's strong compositional moves end up serving more than merely visual ends. The visual energy of his designs does appear to disarm conventional programmes of their intransigent defences. Unusual spaces and unexpected scenes allow us to reinterpret programmes as we see new spatial relationships emerging; the relationship between form and function thus becomes a reciprocal process of criticism, rather than a linear means of determining design.

Since architecture in the end is always a social art, one could say that the visual aspect of architecture reflects to some degree social behaviour. The interest in novelty that characterises Modernism might simply derive from a desire to see evidence of underlying behavioural change. If this is so, then we might look to Pran's fluid, discontinuous compositions to perceive a certain break down in conventional notions of formal hierarchy. Traditionally, the classic architectural approach was to divide given spaces into serving and served spaces; typically this translates into a distinction between rooms of specific function (served space) and corridors linking them (serving space). But today, the corridor, the place of movement, has become more important for daily use, and in an effort to accommodate this change, traditional distinctions between serving and served spaces have been blurred forever. Pran's designs concentrate their greatest impact on these territories of public passage, using curved surfaces to impart an expansiveness and natural dignity to this 'serving' space. His designs inevitably treat the idea of passage as an episodic, fragmentary experience, and this fragmentary aesthetic leads him freely to a multi-centred organisation of programme wholly suited to the complex programmes he tackles. More than being mere visual excitement, however, Pran's energetic proposals for orchestrating buildings around the space of public passage point to a real need for more creative exploration of programme by today's architects and clients.

Kinetic, fragmentary, cinematic – Peter Pran's designs seem to capture something essential about the spirit of this age of complexity and change. We have seen that this kind of complex, fluid composition is far easier to achieve in sculpture, stage art, and interior installations, but it is usually not entirely successful in architecture due to the very intricacies of real functional demands. Peter Pran seems to be one of the few architects up to the challenge of executing convincingly this kind of exciting work in both large and small scale, as a number of recent projects by his deft hand will attest. In an age of intellectual controversy and irony, the poetry of his forms has the ability to silence words and remind us of the ineffable.

PETER PRAN
A Complete Commitment to a Continued and New Modern Architecture

The architectural work presented in this publication expresses a complete commitment both to a continued and new modern architecture and to a new, innovative, explorative, creative, poetic and authentic modern architecture of our times. The tremendous heritage of early modern architecture is the foundation for all substantive contemporary modern architecture. The earlier modern pioneer architects achieved an incredibly wide range of substantive work, often struggling against considerable opposition, to design and realise their progressive and courageous visions. The best modern architecture of today is in many ways substantially different from the earlier modern architecture, but it could not exist without it. Today, it is our challenge and goal to be explorers and creative innovators in a further major development and enrichment of contemporary modern architecture and to chart new courses that will represent our society now and in the future. Experimentation, exploration and theory are the necessary underpinnings, without which no work of major importance can be created. All the great living modern architects show constant and permanent proof in their work that modern architecture provides for the greatest possible richness, diversity and content, for all conceivable building types and all imaginable contexts.

High quality modern architecture developed in countries all over the world brings about the very positive experience of sharing a rich, continued, and new culture; it brings people all over the world closer together. The new modern architecture is defined by a 'site specific' content, and an expressive, poetic feeling of movement and fluency, and the resulting freedom manifests itself in the liberating works produced. In general, the more the external/internal forces on a site are absorbed into the design and creatively responded to – for example, consciousness of history and setting – the better the buildings become. By moving forward and creating a new, progressive, modern architecture, one is exploring new aspects of what it means to be a human being. This progression brings new insight and creates a meaningful environment. Architecture is about giving people the opportunity to live better lives.

The highest creative spirit of modern architecture that we see in the great works of Mies, Le Corbusier, Rietveld and Scarpa has, in most recent years, been carried forward in the great works of Fumihiko Maki, Alvaro Siza, Tadao Ando, Richard Meier, Rem Koolhaas, Ron Krueck, Jean Nouvel, Heikkinen-Komonen, Norman Foster, Esteve Bonell-Francesc Rius, Richard Rogers, Frank Gehry, Jo Coenen, Steven Holl, Snøhetta, Miralles & Pino, Stanley Saitowitz, Luigi Snozzi, Morphosis, Peter Eisenman, Liz Diller & Ricardo Scofidio, Coop Himmelblau, Philippe Starck, Arquitectonica, Arkkitehtuuritoimisto 92/Monark, Bernard Tschumi, Zaha Hadid, Daniel Libeskind, Jörn Utzon, Myron Goldsmith, Fazlur Khan, Peter Cook, Günther Behnisch, IM Pei, Maya Lin, Bowles & Wilson, Zoe Zenghelis, Renzo Piano, Kazuo Shinohara, John Hejduk, Raimund Abraham, Tod Williams & Billie Tsien, Sverre Fehn, Eric Owen Moss, Gwathmey-Siegel, Mack Scogin, Emilio Ambasz, Gustav Peichl and countless other progressive modern architects. There is an exuberant strength and conviction in today's best modern architecture.

The main opposition today is between the new authentic modern architecture and the regressive post-modern (unhistoric) historicism. To try to reverse time and copy historicist motifs in new buildings today undermines society's ability to create its own authentic culture through buildings that represent our own epoch. We all have a compassion for the best buildings built throughout centuries of our history; what modern architects are against is the copying of them today in our completely different times; it degrades the architecture of the past and its superficiality harms today's built environment by not being an expression of our times. However, there is a promising future with many excellent modern architecture students coming out of schools of architecture all over the world, the overwhelming majority of whom are against historicism. For architects today to be backward-looking historicists and anti-modernists of their own choice in their buildings, works directly against our great modern heritage and the further development of an authentic modern architecture of our own times.

Our historical and traditional heritage can be re-interpreted in an authentic contemporary language; we can see it clearly in the best buildings by architects such as Louis Kahn, Frank Lloyd Wright, Le Corbusier and Jean Nouvel (The World Arab Institute, Paris). This referential work represents a completely honest expression of our world today.

Having worked for Mies, the great conviction, strength and commitment to modern architecture that came from him, will always stay with me.

Kenneth Frampton has been the most consistent and superb architectural critic speaking up for modern architecture. He was the first to criticise the Venice Biennale 'Presence of the Past' and the anti-modern books, Robert Venturi's *Complexity and Contradiction in Architecture* and Denise Scott Brown's *Learning from Las Vegas*. Other excellent architects and writers who have in a similar way stood up for modern architecture and must be mentioned are Richard Rogers, Michael Sorkin, Aldo Van Eyck, Michael Rotondi, Juhani Pallasmaa, Ulf Grönvold, Jean Nouvel, Allan Temko, Bruno Zevi, Carl Christiansson, Adele Santos, Joseph Giovannini, Gene Summers, Lars Elton, Pietro Belluschi and Frank Gehry. I admire the clients, architects, critics, and everyone else among the general public who courageously speak up for modern architecture. Politicians, writers, academics, business people and so on, regularly or at appropriate times criticise each other openly; architects likewise have the right to criticise each other when it is justified and this criticism assists the course of architecture. It is important to be tolerant of all good directions in architecture, but tolerance does not mean accepting poor quality design; constructive architectural criticism is always needed in our free society.

JOHN C GAUNT

In music, the visual arts, literature and philosophy, we have all grown greatly in spirit and understanding through the innovative and powerful modern work of individuals such as Philip Glass, Keith Jarrett, Constantin Brancusi, Richard Serra, Paul Klee, Piet Mondrian, Jean Paul Sartre, Bertrand Russell, Franz Kafka, Albert Camus and others. We have all benefited from the struggle of known and unknown individuals working for social justice. In our field of architecture, and within the broadest limits of our profession, it is urgent that a creative, positive, socially concerned, democratic, classless, innovative, informed and courageous architecture of our times be developed, with a passionate care for the future.

Within our firm, Ellerbe Becket, the creative spirit and togetherness of all the project design team members – and the support from the firm at large – are great. While the project teams always pursue a steady progress in design, there is an openness about challenging any idea; every person on the project team has the opportunity to contribute important building design ideas, and if they are the best, they will be used. The exceptional strength of a large firm is that it can continue to grow beyond the life of one leader. The fact that our architecture and engineering firm which is the largest in USA is now considered by the profession to be one that creates leading modern architecture (a fact quite extraordinary for a large firm), is of the greatest pride to all of us in Ellerbe Becket.

The essential goal is that the new modern architecture be accepted and supported everywhere by clients and the general public, and that we as architects communicate with words that are meaningful and intelligible. As Mies' and Le Corbusier's work and influence have been accepted and spread all over the world, it is crucial that all the excellent new modern architecture will spread and be influential and appreciated in all countries, becoming part of the lives of people everywhere.

In the six years that Peter Pran has been with Ellerbe Becket's New York office, he has created a significant body of singularly modernist work that is now reaching fruition in construction. At the same time, he has exerted a remarkable influence within a large and decentralised firm that promises a broader achievement than would be possible from within a smaller practice. Fundamental to this success is the symbiotic combination of a determined personal vision and an organisation that is committed to grow as a positive design force. Ellerbe Becket is organised around the talents of many designers, not an individual or small group of design partners as is more usual. We encourage and develop a diversity of talents in order to respond appropriately to a diversity of clients and to achieve excellence on their behalf. This broad-based approach creates an ideal opportunity for Peter to develop his personal directions in a supportive design environment. Peter and Ellerbe Becket are partners in an ongoing quest to achieve extraordinary modern architecture in a large firm practice. On a personal level, Peter provides an all-too-rare mentorship to the younger architects in the firm. He has taught throughout his career, and has a passionate interest in creating opportunity for young designers which inspires great commitment and loyalty among those who work with him.

John Gaunt is AIA President and President of Ellerbe Becket.

KENNETH FRAMPTON
Ellerbe Becket in New York 1987-92: A Critique

One of the most idiosyncratic features of the New York branch of Ellerbe Becket is the extent to which its practice derives from the architecture of Ivan Leonidov; a fact that is immediately evident from one of the earliest projects of the design team that was formed by Wayne Fishback and Peter Pran in 1986. The fruits of this new beginning first became evident in 1987 when Pran designed a high-rise for South Ferry Plaza, Manhattan, in association with Carlos Zapata. Despite the fact that this 70-storey tower bears little resemblance to Leonidov's skyscraper designs, Pran's turn towards Neo-Suprematism is explicitly revealed through the site plan, which, based on a 6 x 6 square grid, established the conceptual ground against which the high-rise could be read. However, unlike the asymmetrical elevator running up the side of Leonidov's Narkomtiazprom skyscraper of 1933, Pran's tower for the tip of Manhattan was at bottom a symmetrical composition, off-set, by recessed planes and superimposed, pin-wheeling components of various kinds. The resultant form was thus subtly related to the asymmetry of the site, with the ferry terminal to one side and Battery Park to the other. This asymmetrical context was acknowledged without disturbing the axial order of the quasi-Art Deco tower.[1]

That Leonidov was the underlying point of departure for Pran's architecture from this moment on tends to be borne out by his habitual deployment of circular forms, even if the circle in each instance would indicate something quite different. For where in Leonidov a circle in plan invariably meant a sphere or a dome in section, in Pran's architecture a circle was either a topographical demarcation or was developed into a cylinder, as in the somewhat improbable 18-storey museum attached to one corner of the South Ferry tower. Needless to say the tower itself was topped by a cylinder of smaller dimension while the blank base was relieved by a circular Chinese window, through which ferries could gain access to the foot of the tower. All in all, formalism not withstanding, this was a vivacious and deftly proportioned design, one which was regrettably not built given the mediocrity of the average Manhattan high-rise.

The cylinder reappears as a key form in Pran's proposal for the consolidated Schibsted Group, the new combined premises for the *Aftenposten* and *Verdens Gang* newspapers, projected for a downtown site in Oslo in 1988. In this remarkable design the principal cylinder functions both as ground and figure. In the first case it is the atrium that provides light and air to the centre of the block; in the second, it rises above the building as a semi-transparent, ferro-vitreous cylindrical screen within which is suspended an equally translucent cube. This ingenious arrangement sets up a series of striking oppositions; atrium versus urban block, cylinder versus base, cube versus cylinder. This is not the only cylinder however for, as in the South Ferry project, major and minor cylindrical forms also play against each other across the composition; the major being the atrium and the minor being the *batîment d'angle* that carries the mass over the intersection between Akersgaten and Apotekergaten. In what is essentially a piece of traditional urban infill, Pran's Schibsted both employs and denies traditional neo-classical tropes, both the cylindrical atrium and its corresponding cylindrical corner being dematerialised by the contingencies which flank them and by the materials from which they are made. Aside from being totally glazed, both cylinders are relieved by adjacent elements, such as the cube that floats above the atrium or the screen walls fronting onto the aforementioned streets that are tangentially attached to the translucent corner drum.

As one can see from the model, Pran's Schibsted introduces a freshly wrought, tactile palette of materials, that gives substance to the chromatic implications of Leonidov's renderings, so that following El Lissitzky's earlier *Proun* Compositions, certain colours and tones may be said to stand for different materials and their contrasting surface texture.[2] In this regard, Schibsted also recalls Lazlo Moholy-Nagy's Light Modulator of 1925-30,[3] or his later plastic constructions circa 1940,[4] although one could just as easily evoke the contemporaneous work of Naum Gabo, such as his Column 1922-23.[5] That all of this is untapped material drawn from the European avant-garde at the height of its powers between 1920 and 1939 is undeniable, but what is new here is the specific application of its aesthetic density to architectural form. This tactile approach to the *faktura*[6] of contrasting material is further enhanced by the game of treating each facade as semi-autonomous relief construction,[7] so that where the Akersgaten elevation is a warped curtain wall of grey glass and steel, echoing the treatment of the government building across the street, the return elevation on Apotekergaten facade is as the architect put it, ' . . . a different and more complex copper, glass, stone and concrete treatment that is appropriate to the street's more intimate character'.

While the Schibsted project is quite conventional, as far as its detailed spatial planning is concerned, there is no denying the ingenuity of the cylindrical atrium or the inclined elevator that runs up inside the six-storey space in order to give access to the executive offices above; these last being suspended on a square floor plate overlooking the city. It is regrettable that this 'cube' was not, in fact, geometrically rendered as such, for had it been as tall as it is wide, that is to say, only five floors high, it would have obstructed the atrium less and have guaranteed an aerial prospect for all of the executives. This compromise at the level of detail is somehow symptomatic of a weakness lying at the heart of the Pran approach; namely that imagination at times runs ahead of reason with the consequence that a project may be deprived of a full interaction between the two.

Schibsted is followed almost at once by a limited competition for an airline terminal in John F Kennedy International Airport (1988), designed by Pran and Zapata in collaboration with David Leibowitz and Gilbert Balog. Here once again a six-storey cylinder plays a prominent role, not only as a final point of departure and arrival, but also as the initial fulcrum, so to speak, that would allow the rest of the redevelopment to proceed in a logistical sequence. Pran's concept was to employ this cylinder as the transfer point between the terminal and the main rail line coming from the then newly planned transportation centre. In this role it would have fed the rail connections to the new satellite building with its 17 gates and at the same time provided for a ticketing space, until the old terminal could be demolished and replaced. Eventually this cylinder would simply serve all arrivals and departures passing between the transportation centre and the satellite. A bar and a restaurant would be eventually cantilevered into the midst of this glazed volume, thereby affording waiting passengers spectacular views across the apron and the runway. The steel roof over the new terminal, to have been built in the final phase, would not only have served as the key symbol of the whole but also as a foil to the central cylindrical form. Following the lead of Eero Saarinen's TWA terminal (1963), this flat-arched, stressed skin structure surely alluded to the initial thrust of a plane at the point of take-off. This enormous span was projected as housing eight check-in gates on the principal floor with arrivals beneath and bars and restaurants stacked on mezzanines above.

The realisation of a new foyer for the headquarters of the Connecticut firm of Deloitte and Touche (1989) afforded Pran and Zapata an opportunity to demonstrate their culture of materials at a one-to-one scale. Here in a constructivist *tour de force* that demonstrated their ability to re-cast a given circulation space, the architects devised a continuous route leading from the reception entrance area past a conference room and an executive suite, to the main offices of the company. Constantly changing elements were inserted into this procession along its length. Thus the long cantilevered plate-glass reception desk, supported on four steel arms and a single steel column, already suggests the full range of materials that will follow; green tinted glass, brushed stainless steel, copper, mahogany, gun metal, and frosted glass light fittings, together with a black marble floor that would unite the whole. The existing skylight in the original Kevin Roche building afforded a constantly changing pattern of light, reflection and shadow comparable to the kind of sensuous surface that one finds say in Fumihiko Maki's Tepia Building, Tokyo, of approximately the same date. Despite its antecedents, this is surely an arresting expression even if it bears some resemblance to other so-called Deconstructivist works. Judging from the only physical space that has been realised to date, Pran is capable of achieving a level of aesthetic density and control that often seems to escape other practitioners of the 'de-con' line.

However, this sense of balance is not evident to the same degree in every work, as we may judge from the designs for the Minnesota School of Architecture (1988). For while similar tropes reappear with comparable forcefulness such as a toplit atrium serviced by an inclined access stair and an adjacent cylinder containing a library and an auditorium, the subsequent proliferation of surface effects and elements seems totally to overwhelm the dynamic plasticity of the initial *parti*. This is always a risk when one depends unduly on the model as a design tool, for while models can be extremely revealing and even suggestive of certain lines of development, they can also be deceptive from the point of view of scale, leading to a miscalculation as to the amount of articulation necessary to sustain any particular concept.

From 1990 onwards Pran will find himself working on one high-rise development after another and he will bring to this problem the basic *parti* of the split and warped slab, that appears in rudimentary form in the office tower of his Hartford City Hall proposal (1988) and is subsequently elaborated in the Canadian National Royal Trust Building and the so-called Labatts Brewery development, both projected for downtown Toronto between 1989 and 1990. This split high-rise slab will re-emerge as a theme in 1992, in the Corporate Headquarters projected for Jeddah in Saudi Arabia and in a high-rise for a downtown site in The Hague in the Netherlands, designed in the same year. With this particular paradigm, virtually unprecedented save perhaps for Schneider Esleben's Phoenix-Rhein-Rohr building built in Düsseldorf in 1961, everything turns on the sculptural profile of the split slab and on the inflections that modulate its hermetic surface; a recession here, an inclination there, a soft curve in the curtain wall deflecting the axis of the slab and so on. The finest version of this *parti* to date seems to me to be the proposal for The Hague, simply due to the particular plastic contrast that obtains between the two halves of the slab. In some ways perhaps, this Dutch project is the most normative of the various split high-rises that Ellerbe Becket have proposed to date, so that the receding curve of this particular 35-storey slab contrasts in a striking way with the more orthogonal lower block and the adjacent five to six-storey blocks that hold the street line and create an atrium around the main high-rise at grade. It is interesting to note that four different variations of this scheme were presented to the client, each with a slightly different distribution of space and each with a different profile in terms of sculptural character. While the Labatts project of 1990 would be the first occasion on which Ellerbe Becket would employ computer-generated perspectives to such an effective end, Pran's subsequent use of CAD would soon move from the representational to the conceptual, so that different versions of the same assembly could be readily studied as a skeleton morphology, simultaneously demonstrating its various volumetric implications as opposed to the opacity of a relief model, that sooner or later must crystallise into a form that is relatively fixed. With the split slab *parti* much depends on the plastic interplay, not only between the two adjacent slabs but also with regard to the 'third term', namely the spatial element that connects them. And while in The Hague project this third term hardly exists, in Jeddah it has the character of a transparent, crescent-shaped atrium that separates the radial block to the north from the orthogonal slab to the south. Like The Hague, the Corporate headquarters of 1992 incorporates facilities other than those strictly required for administrative purposes, including a mosque, an auditorium and an exhibition space on the ground floor.

The concept of the split-atrium-tower seems to attain its fullest elaboration in Pran's tripartite laboratory designed for the Columbia University Research Center for Disease Prevention in 1991. This project is an elaborate proposition on a number of levels at once; first, because of its contextual response, in which it attempts to modulate its own mass in such a way as to mediate between the five-storey residential stock that flanks it on three sides and the mass of the 20-storey Columbia Presbyterian Medical Center that runs along Broadway to the west; second, because its spatial matrix is inflected in such a way as to register the fact that it lies at an intersection between the diagonal of Broadway and the orthogonal city grid; and finally, because it breaks down into three separate components on a trapezoidal site. Projected around an open atrium these three elements and their corner conditions create a dynamic spatial complexity that is further enriched by flying bridges connecting the inner gallery circulation at different levels. This complex interaction is reflected in the treatment of the outer membrane that aside from being warped and recessed at certain points is also finished in different materials, ranging from tinted and transparent glass, to copper, anodised metal, stack bonded brickwork and stone sheathing. The exact make-up and juxtaposition of this mix was left open given the preliminary status of the design. However, this proposal is of interest in other respects, first because two equally interesting versions were projected for the same site and programme and second, and more significantly from a methodological viewpoint, because two alternative 'relief constructions' were arrived at through the use of CAD modelling, with computer-generated perspectives being taken from different angles, including an aerial shot and a dramatic upward view of the atrium. Equally significant was the way in which CAD enabled the office to gain greater control over the projection of the building as a relief construction. Thus what was previously indicated by a change in material literally applied to a cardboard or wooden model now becomes the representation of a surface inflection that was easily superimposed on the three dimensional co-ordinates of the complex as a whole. This not only assures higher levels of resolution throughout but also maintained a volumetrical fluidity that enabled the architect to modify the work in process while keeping creative track of all the ramifications of any particular change. While this may appear to be nothing more than a superior method of model manipulation it evidently leads to aesthetically different results. These seem to arise, almost spontaneously, from the greater precision of the spatial articulation and representation. It points to a fundamental difference that separates a mastery of CAD technique from a subservience to its operational constraints. We cannot conclude our discussion of Pran's Columbia proposal, however, without commenting on the way in which certain tropes are seemingly taken over here from an earlier phase of the practice, such as the cubic penthouse that in the first version of the research laboratory recalls the aerial cube of the Schibsted proposal or the warping and exfoliating of the skin that in all its manifestations, as rendered by CAD, reminds one of nothing so much as Jakob Chernikov's air-brushed *Architectural Fantasies* executed between 1929 and 1933, that, in their turn, owed much to Leonidov and even more to the imaginative projections of the UNOVIS school, that is to say to the Suprematism of Malevich and the elaborations of his immediate pupils Klutsis, Suetin and Lissitzky.

Neo-Suprematism is again latent in the new facility projected in 1992 for the State University of New York at Binghamton. Housing three new faculties dedicated to management, nursing and education, this academic in-fill building has been conceived as a 'portal', offering a new and more contained mode of access from the campus ring-road to the existing science quadrangle. Appearing in plan as a collage of 'footprints', rather arbitrarily drawn from the split-tower *parti*, this gateway building ties together a number of pedestrian routes, both inside and out. In this instance the computer-generated perspectives make one realise only too keenly how the glazed prow of the admissions wing and the equally transparent entrance to the school of education would interact about a threshold, laid out as a rectangular paved area. In fact the idea of a split structure is doubly present in this work, first in the plans of the buildings themselves and then in the gap between the crescent-shaped block and the inflected rectilinear bar housing the faculty of education. At the same time, a conscientious effort was made to relate the dematerialised character of this complex to the general massing and block height of the existing campus.

This penultimate design, like the large hospital that Pran recently projected for Norway or the small urban banks designed by the office for Ecuador in 1992, brings one to the difficult task of evaluating the ultimate stature of the work, compelling one to pass from the ostensible intent of the architect to a consideration of the nature of the work. One is thus brought to ask to what degree may we regard this remarkable output, comprising no less than 20 projects in five years, as being of a Deconstructivist character? No document can perhaps be of more assistance to us, in an attempt to answer the question, than the catalogue of the *Deconstructivist Architecture* exhibition, staged in the Museum of Modern Art in 1988, from which the early work of the Ellerbe office was excluded.

To imply the closeness of the expression of the office to Deconstruction as a style, albeit difficult to define, is to acknowledge at least that the practice has long since distanced itself from the dematerialised minimalist geometry of Leonidov in his prime and from Pran's own Miesian formation at IIT. Instead we can perhaps say that it has drawn somewhat closer to the transrational, science-fiction space, that was implied by the Neo-Suprematist Proun.[6] As a result Pran refuses to embrace the cacophonous, disjunctive free-for-all that seems, at times, to have become the touchstone of the Deconstructionist mode, as we find it say in the most recent work of Eric Owen Moss or Mack

Scogin, to cite only two progenitors of today's American 'deconstructivist' practice. Approaching the most recent work of Peter Eisenman where the envelope is highly organic but the plans remain somewhat normative as in say Eisenman's project for a highly performing arts center at Emery University, Pran's spatial organisation is of an equally measured and dialectal kind. In this respect he is in the habit of reserving his more dynamic spatial sequences for the servant sector, that is to say, for the circulation, leaving the *served* volume relatively passive in its disposition and often orthogonal in terms of its planimetric organisation. Aside from the spatial fracturing of the circulation space, Pran's inflections invariably take place at a micro-scale, in plan, interrupting the otherwise smooth surface of a curtain wall, or at the macro-level in section, where the disjunction takes the form of an asymmetrical flat-arched roof as in the JFK airline terminal or the Minnesota architectural school. Indeed just such a roof will emerge as the primary trope in the Ecuadorian banks and in the McCormick Place stadium, projected for Chicago in 1991. Indeed the banks in question would barely exist as architectural propositions were it not for their low seeping roofs and it is significant that it is only in these works that structure in a tectonic sense comes into its own; that is to say, here for the first time in Pran's practice, columnar structure is allowed to be fully expressive in conjunction with the beam and roof system that it supports. In all of this, of course, we could not be further from the Neo-Suprematist atectonic *tachisme* of an architect like Daniel Libeskind or from the equally wilful, over-stressing of structural fabric that has by now become the acrobatic mode of Zaha Hadid. Far from participating in an aestheticism that is self-indulgent and inadvertently oppressive, Pran's architecture still seems to intend a modernity that is liberative in all its aspects. A number of lacunae remain, however, not least of which is the need to develop an appropriate spatial methodology for achieving a smooth passage between the normative and the dynamically inflected aspects of his work. I have in mind a kind of taxonomic-spatial elision such as we find say in the *plan libre* of Le Corbusier or in the heterotopic methodology of Alvar Aalto, but which seems to be largely absent say, in the rather rigid planning of the Rikshospital proposed by Pran for Oslo in 1990. The computer-generated perspectives produced in order to represent this particular work also lead one to pause since they illustrate how readily cybernetic images may also induce a kind of self-deception; of a different order from that of the scale model but no less misleading.

Looking back over this remarkably diverse production it seems barely credible that so much work could have been produced over such a short period of time. That almost all of this exceptionally imaginative output remains unrealised to date, testifies not only to the stature of the average client in a reactionary period of history, but also to the remarkable morale of Pran and his design team that have, on so many occasions, displayed the prerequisite stamina and talent to go from one *charette* to the next; to take on yet another demanding client or competition, to face yet another conservative planning board and to suffer yet another disappointment due to failures of nerve of various kinds. Without Pran's astonishing energy, vision and determination, few of these projects would have come into being, for architecture when it is not merely the stuff of everyday commerce, is surely contingent on vision and passion. To take this calibre of work even to schematic design requires total commitment notwithstanding repeated setbacks and misunderstandings and the necessity of often having to swallow one's pride. As Alvaro Siza puts it so pithily, an architect who gives the client what he or she wants is demagogue for the architect must learn from the client, but also the client must learn from the architect, for the client is invariably misinformed and inevitably this leads to an abrasive situation. In recent years perhaps few architects have had to become so habituated with confrontation as Peter Pran, but now at long last this arduous strategy seems to be paying off at least for Ellerbe Becket in New York for they are now beginning to build on a large scale. More importantly in the long run this strategy is beginning to influence one of the largest architectural offices in the world, namely, the parent company of Ellerbe Becket in Minneapolis where the production is beginning to improve, due in part it would seem to the influence of its New York office. For all the volatile make-up of the talented team that is at his side, Pran has so far never wavered from his revision of modernity, from his return to a gossamer-like 'almost nothing' of a different order from that of Mies van der Rohe whom he once served so faithfully in Chicago. It is to be hoped that when it comes to the detailing of this architecture, as it soon will with the 1992 Corporate Headquarters in Jeddah proposal, Pran will look once again to the Germans rather than to the high fashion of the Anglo-American transatlantic line, that is to say, that he will look back to the Weimar Mies and forward, so to speak, to the refinement of an architect like Günther Behnisch who has shown perhaps more explicitly than other contemporary architects, the full poetic potential of a well constructed de-construction.

Notes

1 There is certain resemblance of this design to the second esquisse made by George Howe and William Lescaze for the PSFS Building in Philadelphia, dated 20 March 1929. This is not to suggest that there is any influence of the one on the other but rather to note the common pseudo-Art Deco character. See Robert Stern, *George Howe*, Yale University Press, 1975, fig 60.

2 See for example El Lissitzky's *Proun 1A, Bridge 1*, 1919, in *El Lissitzky: Life, Letters, Text*, Thames & Hudson, London, 1968, text by Sophie Lissitzky Küppers.

3 I am referring to the mechanised mobile of chromium steel and glass used by Moholy-Nagy to project abstract light-shadow sequences in his film *Light Play, Black-White-Grey*. See S Moholy-Nagy, *Moholy-Nagy: Experiment in Totality*, MIT Press, Cambridge, Massachusetts, 1969, pp 64-67.

4 Such as *Mills No: 2* by L Moholy-Nagy, Plexiglass Space-Modulator. See *Moholy-Nagy: Experiment in Totality*, fig 58.

5 *Column 1922-23* is a vertical abstract construction made of glass, perspex and stainless steel. Another version was made in 1975. See *Naum Gabo, Sixty Years of Constructivism*, Prestel-Verlag, 1985, p 100, fig 11.

6 See Christina Lodder, *Russian Constructivism*, Yale University Press, London & New Haven, 1983, pp 94-95. In giving an account of the argument advanced in Alexi Gan's manifesto *Constructivism* of 1922, Lodder writes:

> The basis for this 'communistic expression of material structures' was the conversion of 'the specific elements of reality', ie tectonics, construction and *faktura*, into volume, plane, colour, space and light. The tectonic (*tektonika*) was defined as emerging from the ideological tenets of communism on the one hand and, on the other, from the appropriate use of industrial metals. Construction (*konstruktsiva*) represented the process of structuring and organising these materials, and *faktura* was the conscious working of the material and using it in an expedient manner without hampering the tectonic or the construction.

While this definition of the period may seem to be somewhat tautological, Lodder will also show elsewhere how the term *faktura* alluded to the specific and often contrasting *texture* of the material construction. She cites Waldemar Matvey's writing in 1914 of the structural form of the traditional Russian icon to the effect that ' . . . Through the resonance of the colours, the sound of the materials, the assemblage of textures . . . the real world is introduced into (the icon's) creation only through the assemblage and incrustation of real tangible objects. And this seems to produce a combat between two worlds, the inner and outer.' See also Margit Rowell 'Vladimir Tatlin: Form/Faktura', *October* No: 7, 1978, p 94. The term 'culture of materials' has its origin in the Institute for Artistic Culture or INKhUK founded in 1921.

While I am not suggesting that Pran was consciously aware of any of this specific history, I feel that it is necessary to introduce such terminology in discussing his work.

7 In his book *Die Kunstismen 1914-1924* El Lissitzky will write: 'These artists look (at) the world through the prisma of technic. They don't want to give an illusion by the means of colours on canvas, but work directly in iron, wood, glass, a.o . . .'

SOUTH FERRY PLAZA
Manhattan, New York, USA, 1987

Placed partly on land and partly on water, the building defines the edge condition and is necessarily asymmetrical to respond to the asymmetrical urban setting. The exterior expresses the main, varied functions creating a strong link and extension to New York City's skyscraper design heritage. The 75-storey highrise contains offices, conference centres and a TV/Radio station at the top, while the cylindrical intersecting building contains a museum.

Architects: *Peter Pran and Carlos Zapata*
Assistant: *Maria Wilthew*
Consultant: *Ellerbe Becket*

SITE PLAN

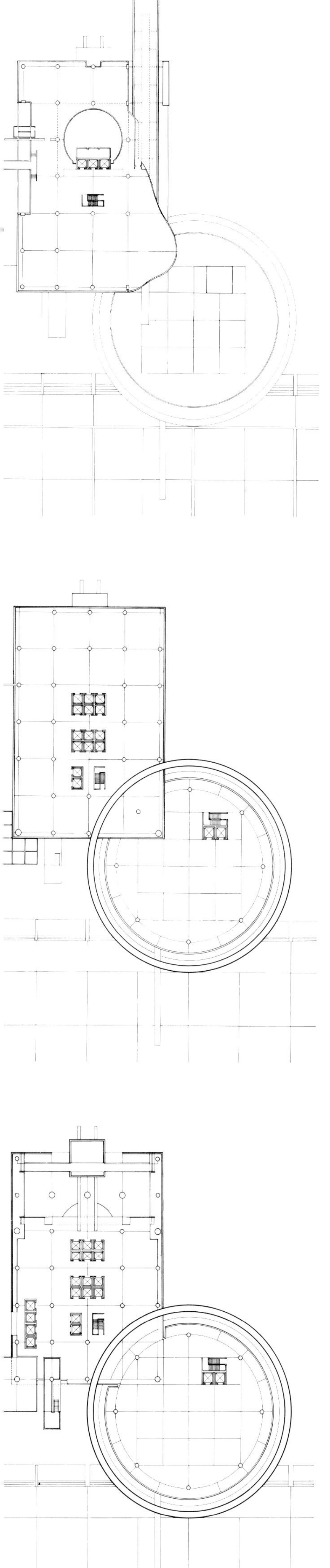

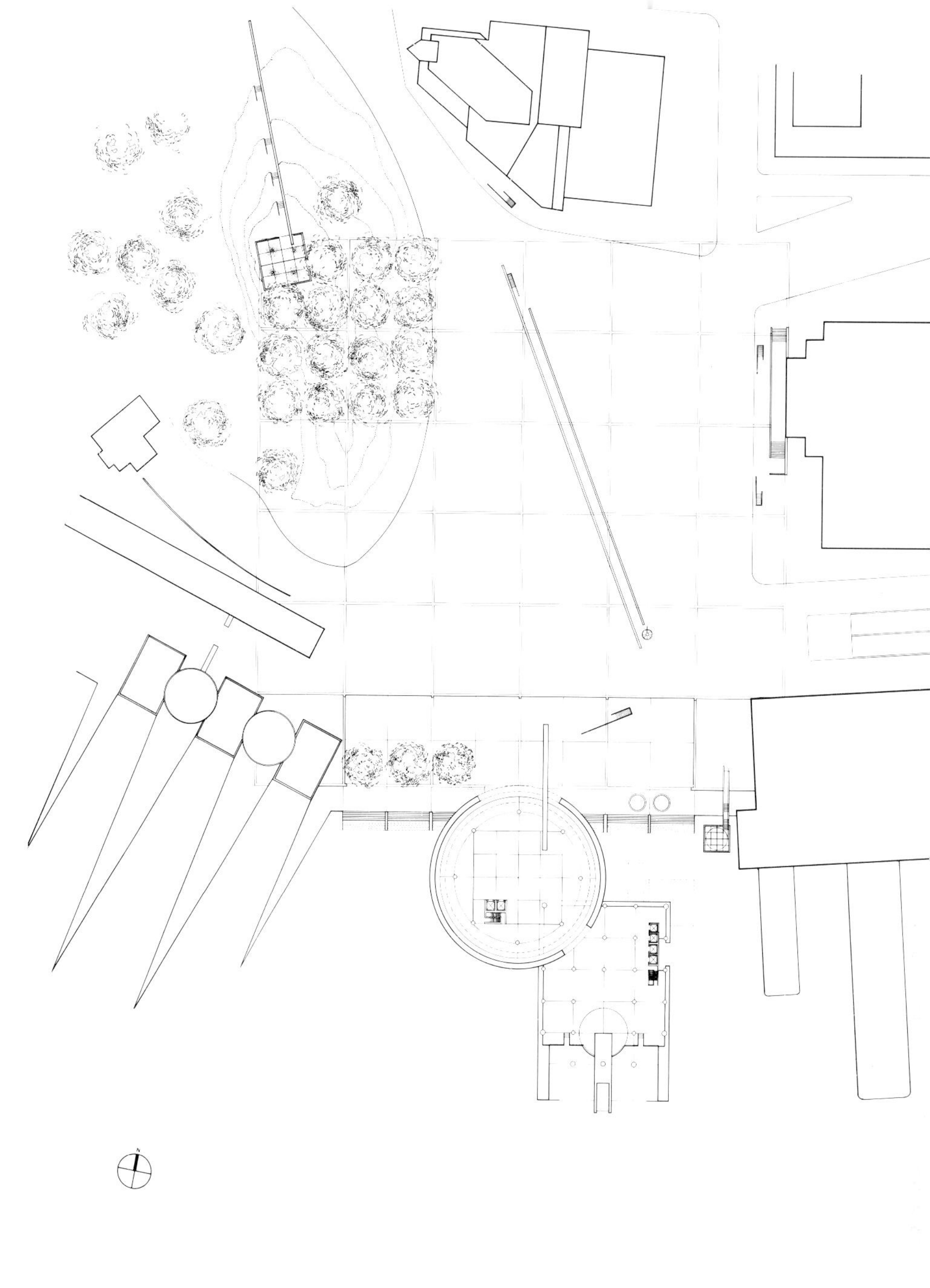

CONFERENCE CENTRE PLAN, FLOOR 41
TYPICAL OFFICE-MUSEUM PLAN, FLOORS 7-15
ELEVATOR TRANSFER PLAN, FLOOR 6

GROUND FLOOR PLAN

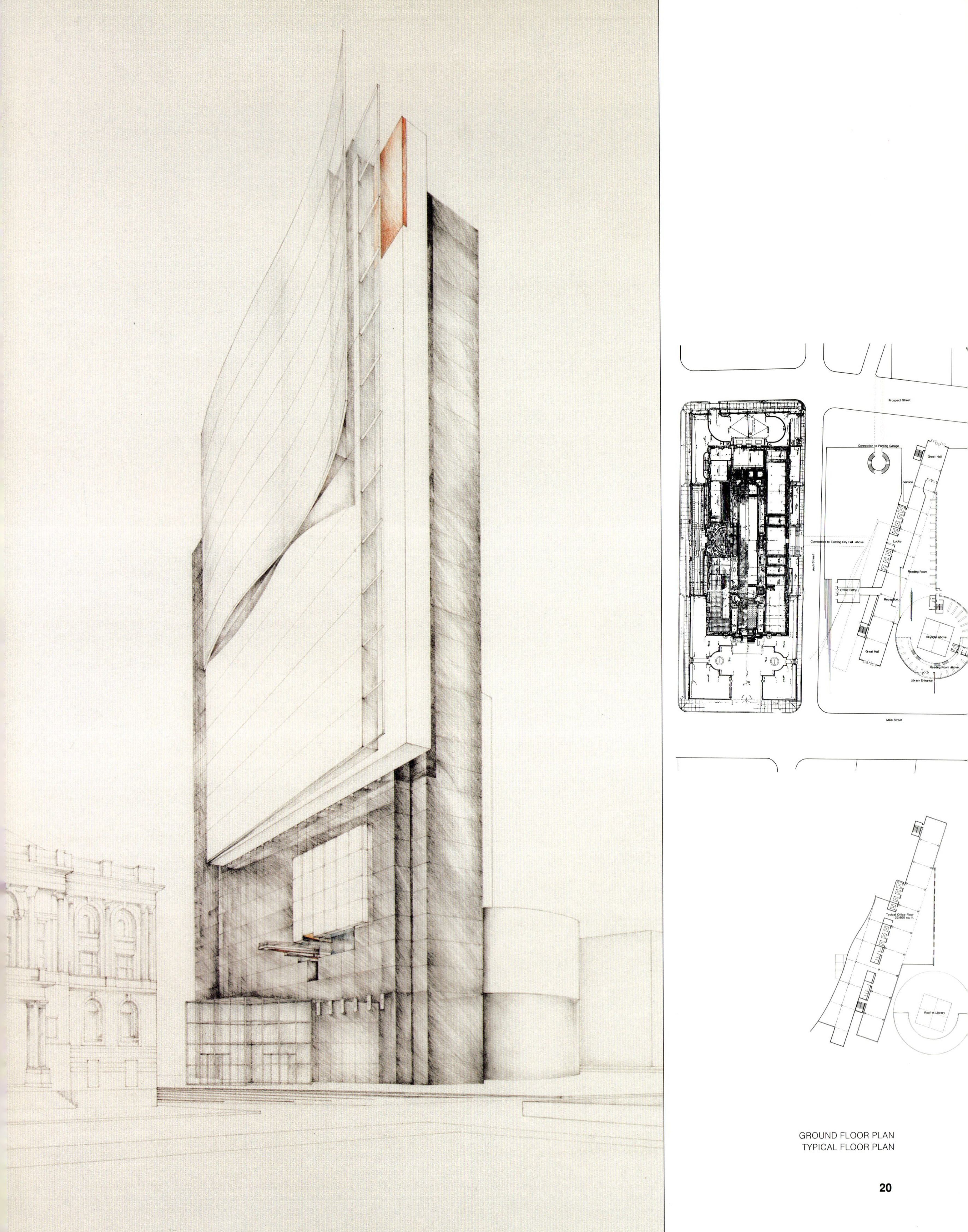

GROUND FLOOR PLAN
TYPICAL FLOOR PLAN

NEW HARTFORD CITY HALL
Hartford, Connecticut, USA, 1988

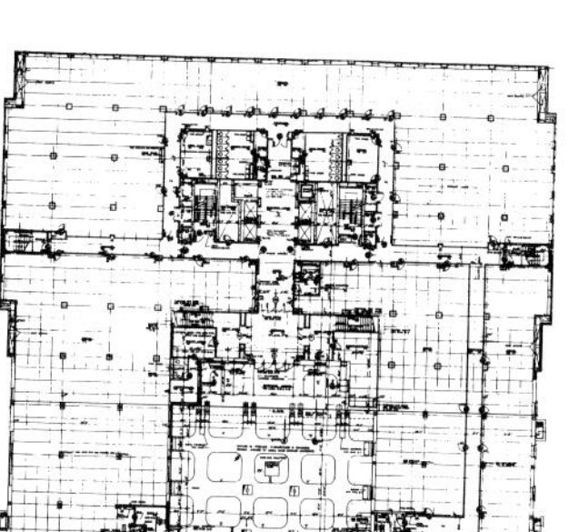

The 25-storey modern contemporary highrise office building will serve as the new city hall, with the existing old neo-classical city hall serving as the ceremonial centre for the city. By designing this modern highrise and not mimicking the style of the old city hall, the contrast between the old and new city halls makes both buildings stand out, with their respective architectural qualities made more significant. As a complex, the new and old buildings give each other strength.

The new city hall buildings are given frontage to Main Street and a direct visual connection with the Capitol and the City Park. The building complex is tilted to allow a new round library design to be incorporated with the office building and to open the exterior space between the new and the old city halls. The tilt also accentuates the intersection of the Main Street axis and the axis of the highway below, and gives the new building a pointed direction towards the Capitol and the City Park. The tilt gives the office building a free and non-static quality, while a wing of the highrise is hinged out and placed parallel to the city streets thereby relating to the city grid.

A glass cube on the plaza level defines the main storey and contains the entry lobby. Inside the long black building block on the ground floor, is a four-storey high 'great hall' that runs the entire length of the building.

It is essentially a wall building, articulated in vertical layers of central office space and vertical transportation. From the main 'building wall', additional upper office floors are cantilevered over the main entry. The typical upper office has a narrower width than a typical speculative office floor, and thereby gives window space to all employees. It is a building full of movement and creative tension. The layering of interior spaces is rich and varied. The black central wall building accents its central role articulating the white cantilevered upper floors over the entry cube and also the exterior entry space between the old and the new city halls. The black glass wall further stands in contrast to the old white stone-clad city hall, and makes the fine articulation of each building even more pronounced.

Client: City of Hartford
Architects: Ellerbe Becket: Peter Pran, Design Principal and Senior Vice President; Carlos Zapata, Senior Project Designer; B Wayne Fishback, Project Director and Senior Vice President
Model: Jessie Rodriques
Consulting Architects: Arthur Lubetz
Contractor: O&G Industries: Maurice Hoben, Partner

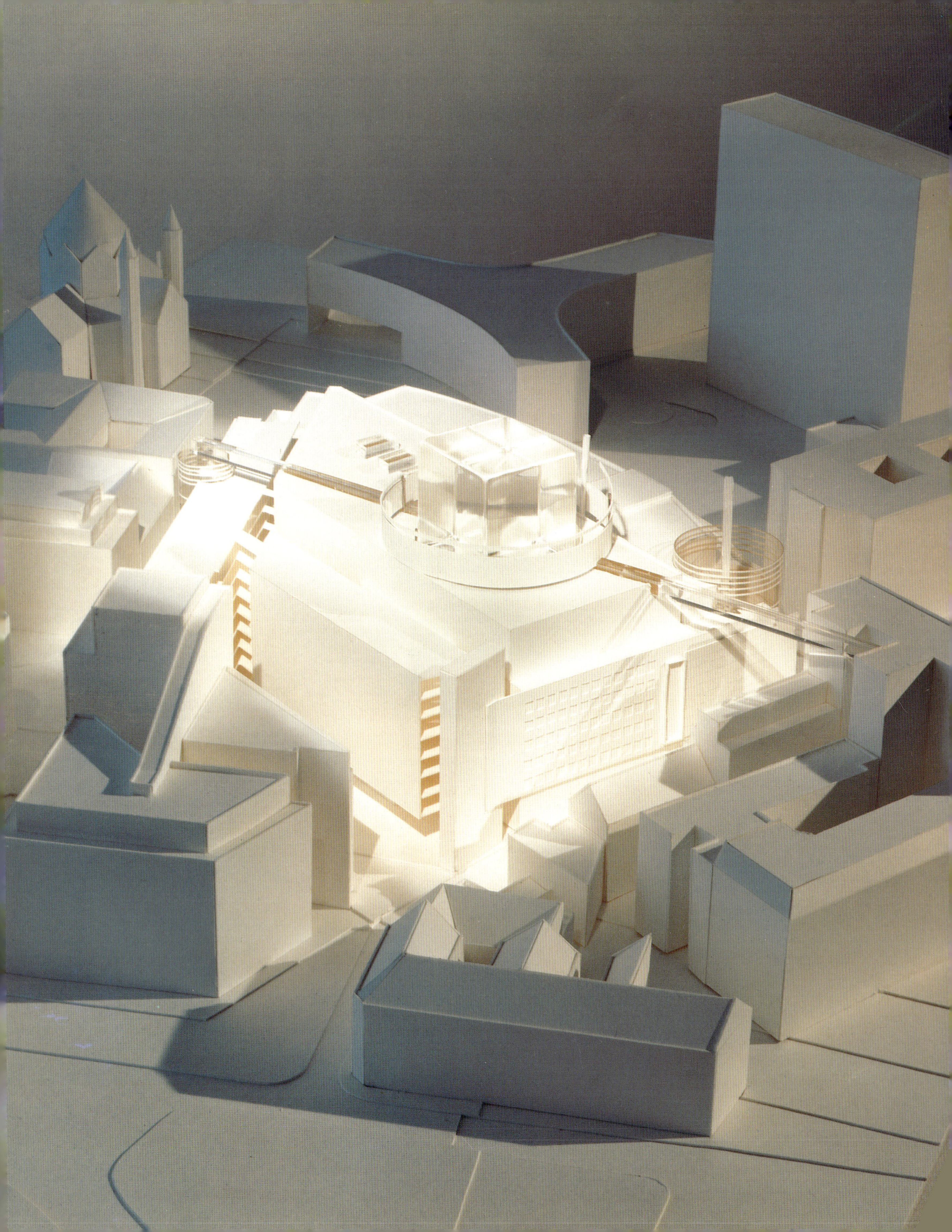

DITTEN PROJECT FOR SCHIBSTED GRUPPEN NEWSPAPER HEADQUARTERS
Oslo, Norway, 1988

This design is the first prize winner in an international/national architecture competition. The building will be the new headquarters for Aftenposten and Verdens Gang, the two largest newspapers in Norway. The building site is located along Akersgaten, the main newspaper street in Oslo, adjacent to the two existing newspaper buildings. The site is located across the street from three main Government Buildings and two blocks away from the Parliament Building, Karl Johans Gate and Studenterlunden, the area which in many ways constitutes the heart of the city. Schibsted Gruppen, our client, owns both the two newspapers.

The exuberant entry space and the highly articulated exterior entry celebrate and dignify the approach and arrival into the headquarters for these two important newspapers. Although the vertically shaped cylinder entry space defines a corner entry, an asymmetrical arrangement in massing and facades relates appropriately to the two different streets it is facing. The facade towards the main street Akersgaten is given a rich, horizontal expression in glass and steel, respectful of the height and character of the government building across the street. The long facade facing the side street Apotekergaten is given a different and more complex copper-glass-stone-concrete treatment that is appropriate for the street's more intimate character. The entry cylinder receives these two facades and pulls them together by allowing vertical and horizontal elements and enclosed spaces to intersect and move through it. Along Teatergaten and Munch's Gate, the building masses are pulled out as individual blocks or 'walls' defining the overall complex along these streets. The separation of these two building blocks also allows them to be rented out apart from the major portion of the complex. The centre of this unusual and idiosyncratic building site is defined by a large cylindrical atrium giving one the feeling of having 'arrived'. Within this cylinder is suspended a floating cube, that houses the main staff cafeteria at its top, with a magnificent view of the entire City of Oslo. The cube is held up structurally by two asymmetrically placed columns, with an elevator on a slant attached in tracks to one of these. A diagonal walkway on the ground floor connects the main entries at the corner of Akersgaten/Apotekergaten and the corner of Teatergaten/Munch's Gate, while intersecting the central cylindrical atrium. The articulated exterior facades give the two newspapers a new image. The metal-glass-stone facades continue the modern character of the existing Aftenposten and Verdens Gang buildings.

Our responsibility is to contribute to the cultural life and values of the City of Oslo. The goal is to attempt to achieve an authentic contemporary building; a building that is not static, but expresses movement and complexity as an expression of our own time and lives.

Client: Schibsted Gruppen, Verdens Gang and Aftenposten: Einar Fr Nagell-Erichsen; Alexander Huitfelt; Stein Föyen; Erik Furevik; Kjell Aamot, VG; Geir Andersen, VG; Arne Tunheim, Aftenposten

Client Representative/Project Manager: Egil Vedal

Architect: Ellerbe Becket, New York: Peter Pran, Design Principal and Senior Vice President; Carlos Zapata, Senior Project Designer and Associate Design Director; B Wayne Fishback, Senior Vice President, Administrative Principal; Curtis Wagner, Project Designer; Eduardo Calma, Project Designer; Vatche Aslanian, Designer; Maria Wilthew, Project Designer; Robert Zumwalt, Chief Architect/Production; Michael Welebit, Project Manager

Model Photographer: Dan Cornish, ESTO

Associate Architect: Platou, Oslo, Norway: Jan Digerud, Partner; Jon Ronning, Partner; Henrik Arentzen, Technical Coordinator

Photographer: Dan Cornish

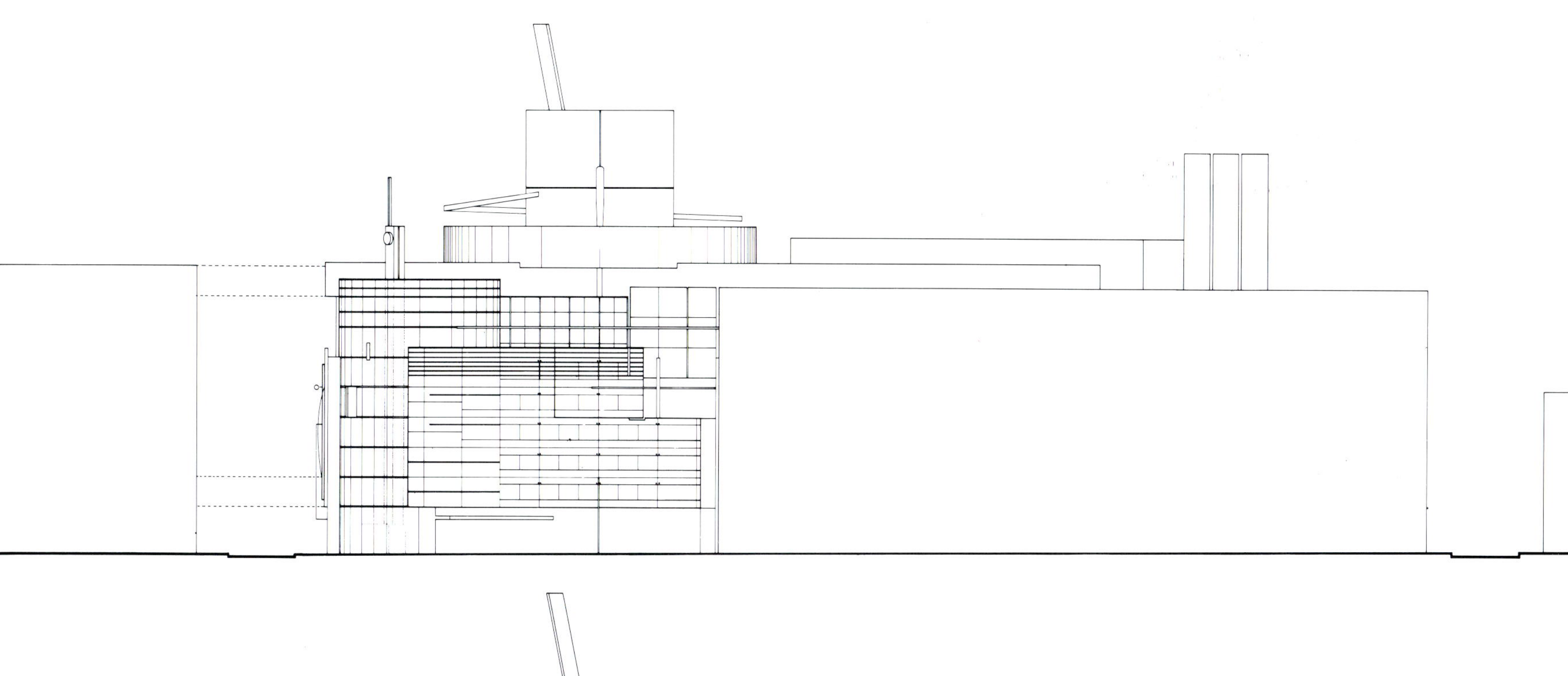

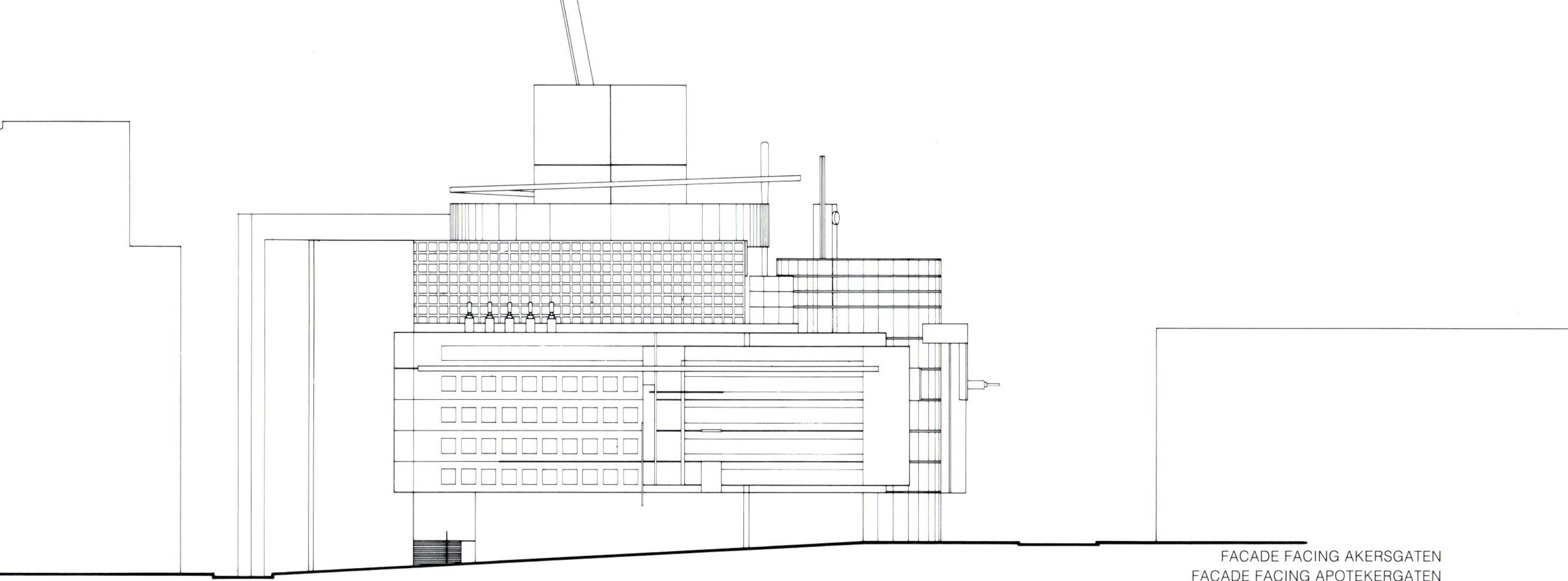

FACADE FACING AKERSGATEN
FACADE FACING APOTEKERGATEN

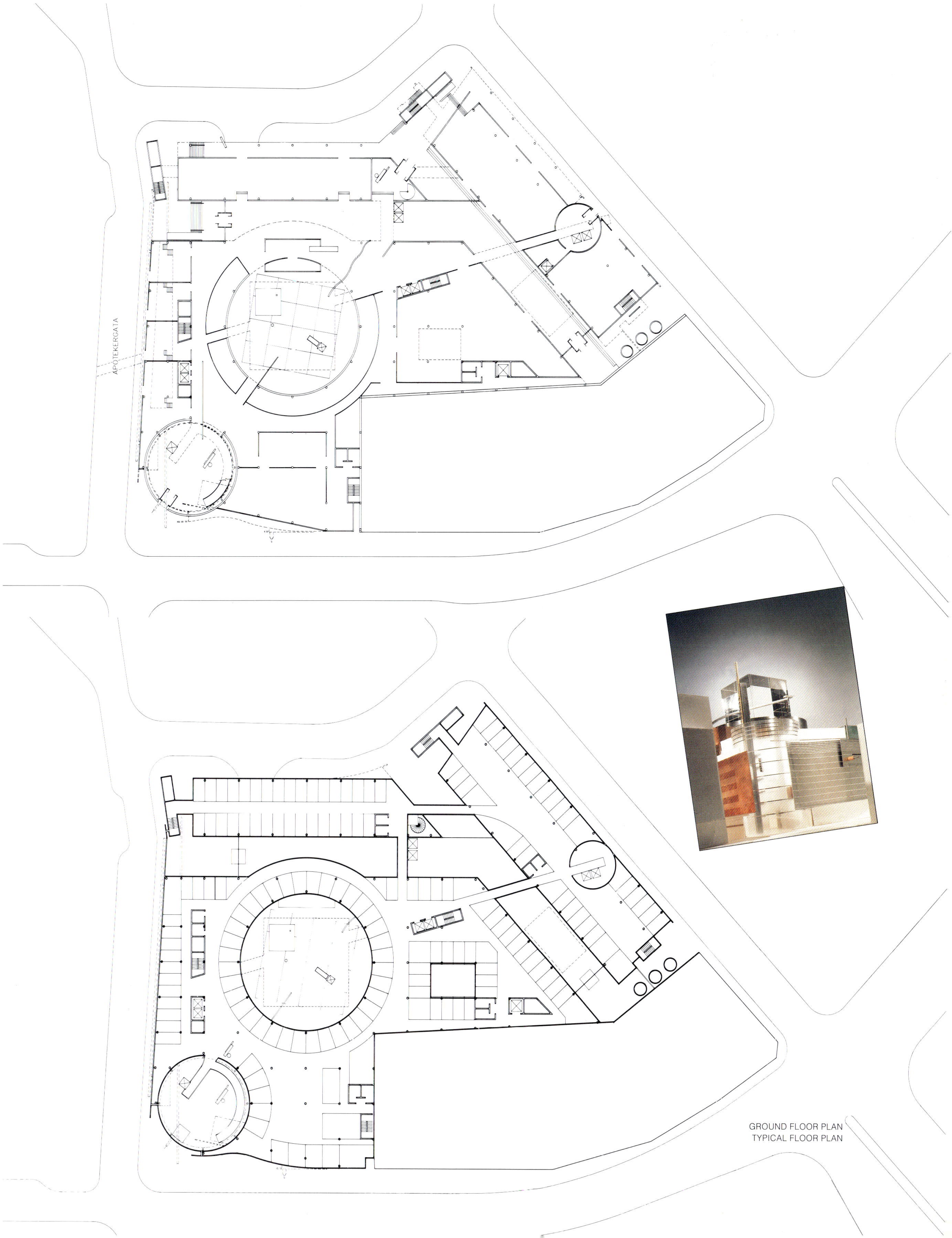
ÅPOTEKERGATA
GROUND FLOOR PLAN
TYPICAL FLOOR PLAN

CONSOLIDATED TERMINAL FOR AMERICAN AIRLINES/NORTHWEST AIRLINES JOHN F KENNEDY INTERNATIONAL AIRPORT

New York, USA, 1988

One of five finalists in the international architectural competition, this is the design for the new $600 million American Airlines/Northwest Airlines Terminal Building at JFK Airport in New York, the first new terminal to be built at JFK for 30 years.

The new AA/NA Terminal will, when fully developed, provide 44 aircraft gates. Approximately 13 gates will handle 747 aircraft; 80 per cent of the traffic will be for international flights and 20 per cent for domestic flights. International flights require Federal Inspection Services (FIS). To provide the maximum number of gates, one part of the new terminal will be a satellite allowing for a layout that accommodates 44 gates, and also two 747 taxi-ways between the main terminal and the satellite.

This new AA/NA Terminal will fit into the JFK 2000 Master Functional Plan, and fit in with the new Transportation Centre and Passenger Distribution System. Small, automatic trains, holding 80 to 200 people at one time, will bring passengers directly to and from the Transportation Centre to the new AA/NA Terminal in 1993.

This innovative planning layout, with all support services and amenities, provides customers with the best possible, hassle-free experience, that will soon begin to attract new passengers in its own right. The overall design has as its main statement and strength a long, curved, floating steel roof that seems to come out of the ground; it spans over the entire arrival and departure area. This elegantly and delicately detailed steel roof expresses a poetic statement of movement and flight. The design creates a feeling of anticipation and delight in the passengers and celebrates the many aspects of flying.

The glass cylinder, placed adjacent to the flying steel roof, contains the arrival/departure station for the automatic trains/vehicles going to and from the Transportation Centre, as well as the arrival/departure station for the automatic trains moving back and forth between the main terminal and the satellite. In addition, the glass cylinder contains a special bar and restaurant that cantilever out into the large, round, interior atrium. From this restaurant people will have a panoramic view of all the aeroplanes arriving and departing.

In the main part of the terminal, the part that is covered and enclosed by the large floating steel floor, are placed the arrival and departure floors. The departure level contains ticketing as well as concession stands. Above this floor, on the mezzanine level are located restaurants and bars.

Most of the existing terminals at JFK Airport, with one exception, are representative of a more static modern architecture of the 1950s-60s, the exception being the TWA terminal designed by Eero Saarinen, with its beautiful central interior space. A large number of airport terminals around the world look like suburban office buildings. This new AA/NA Terminal seems to fit in with total grace and respect for the setting at JFK Airport. The design embraces the existing airport and also brings out its full architectural potential.

Client: American Airlines/Northwest Airlines, Port Authority of New York and New Jersey
Architects: Leibowitz/Ellerbe Becket; Ellerbe Becket, New York: Peter Pran, Senior Vice President, Principal -in-Charge; Carlos Zapata, Associate Design Director and Vice President; B Wayne Fishback, Senior Vice President; Administrative Principal; Curtis Wagner, Project Designer; Eduardo Calma, Project Designer; Frank Yu, Designer; Maria Wilthew, Designer; Darius Sollohub, Designer; Vatche Aslanian, Designer; The Office of David Elliot Leibowitz: David Leibowitz, President, Principal-in-Charge; Gilbert E Balog, Senior Vice President, Principal-in-Charge of Programming and Planning; James Robinson, Planner; Mohammed Reza Samii, Planner; Albert Henning, Planner; Antonio Rodriquez, Planner; Keith Doble, Planner
Photographer: Dan Cornish

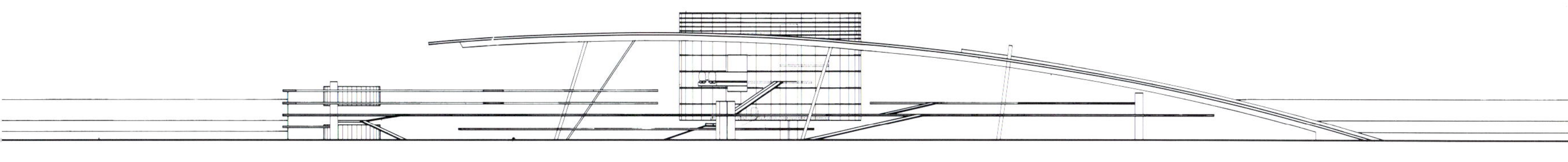

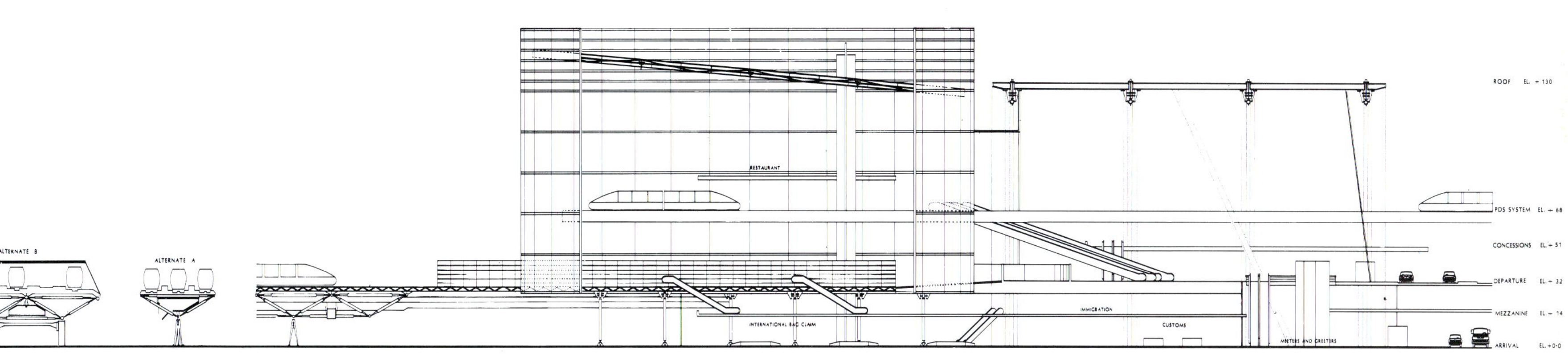

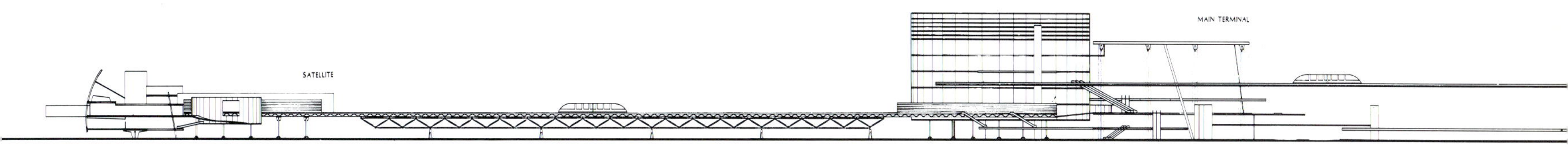

LONGITUDINAL SECTION
TRANSVERSE SECTION
TRANSVERSE SECTION

SITE PLAN

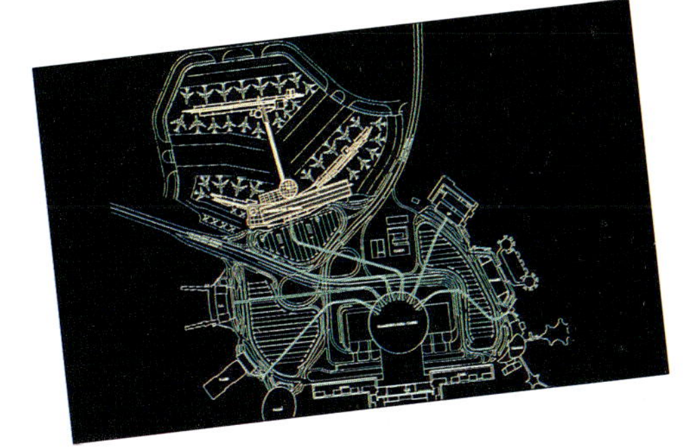

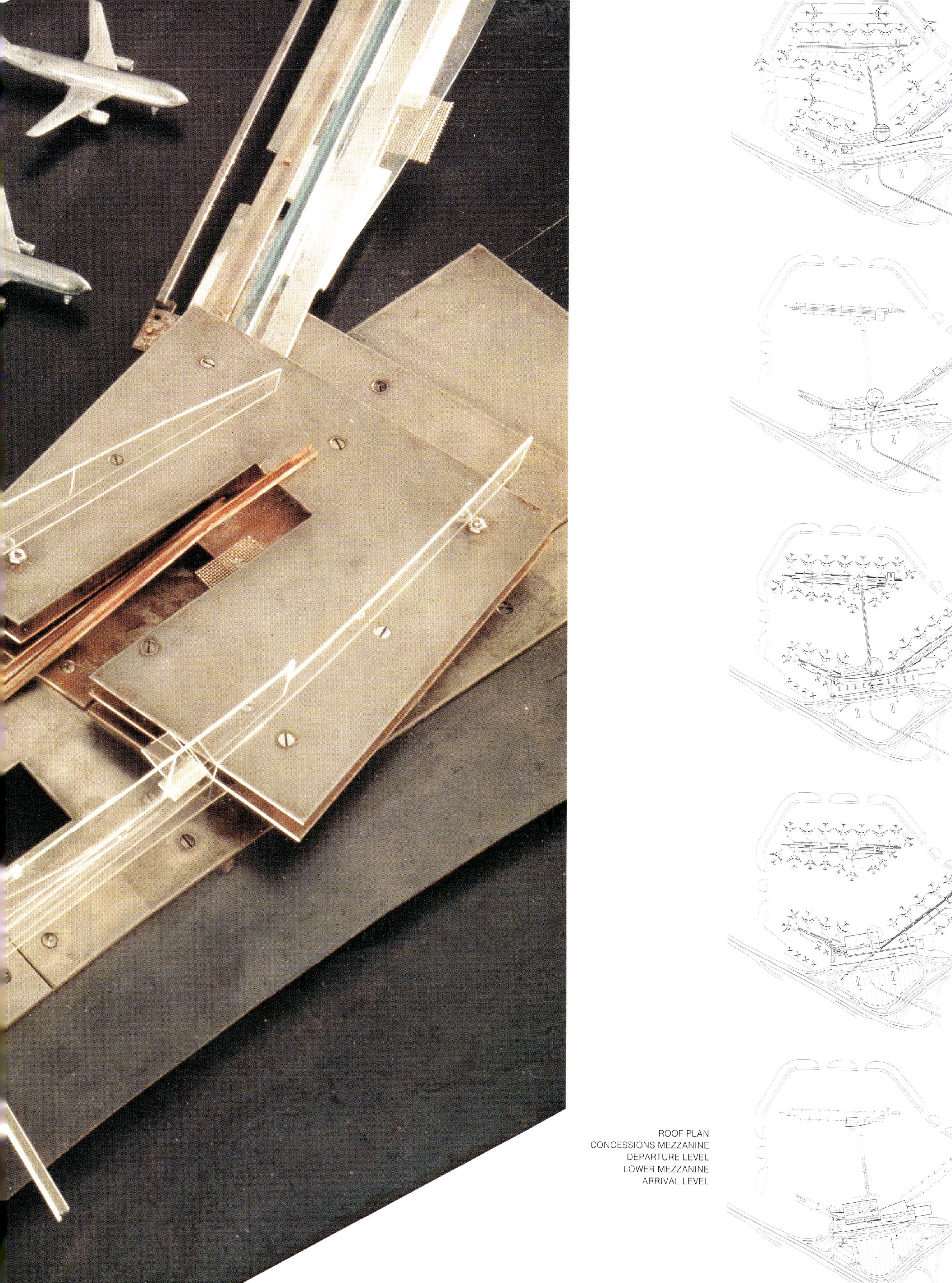

ROOF PLAN
CONCESSIONS MEZZANINE
DEPARTURE LEVEL
LOWER MEZZANINE
ARRIVAL LEVEL

DELOITTE & TOUCHE HEADQUARTERS EXECUTIVE AREA
Wilton, Connecticut, USA, 1989

This project is the result of a carefully controlled juxtaposition of new functionally derived architectural elements over the structure of an existing Kevin Roche 1960's building.

The product is a sequence of elegant spaces enclosed among remaining structural corners and a sequentially located flowing layer of new architectural elements. Walls, partitions, lighting fixtures and furniture slide past one another without touching, in this way giving the space a sense of continuity and allowing natural light to filter from space to space.

The procession from entry to back offices begins with a long glass reception desk supported by four curving steel ribs cantilevered from the floor. Above the desk is a long skylight that runs the entire length of the offices forming part of the original design of the building. All remaining elements are organised diagonally along the skylight attached to and suspended from floors, ceilings and walls, in this way creating a well-balanced procession for the visitor to experience. The selection of materials and the high quality of craftsmanship existing throughout, give the project an image which is forward-looking and sophisticated.

This project successfully incorporates many diverse uses including a TV studio, training facilities, management and client areas, a state-of-the-art reception area, board room and senior partner offices with support services.

Client: *Deloitte & Touche: Jerry Kolb, Vice Chairman; Gregory J O'Connell, Manager, National Facilities*
Architect: *Ellerbe Becket, New York: Peter Pran, Senior Vice President and Design Principal; Carlos Zapata, Vice President and Associate Design Director; Ed Calma, Project Designer; B Wayne Fishback, Administrative Partner; Maria Wilthew, Designer; Curtis Wagner, Designer; Frank Yu, Designer; Carol Krewson, Project Director; Michael Welebit, Project Manager; Arch Currie, Project Manager; Michael Rufino; Moon Kim; Carol Napper; Ron Miranda*
Photographers: *Dan Cornish, Chuck Choi, Wayne Fujii*

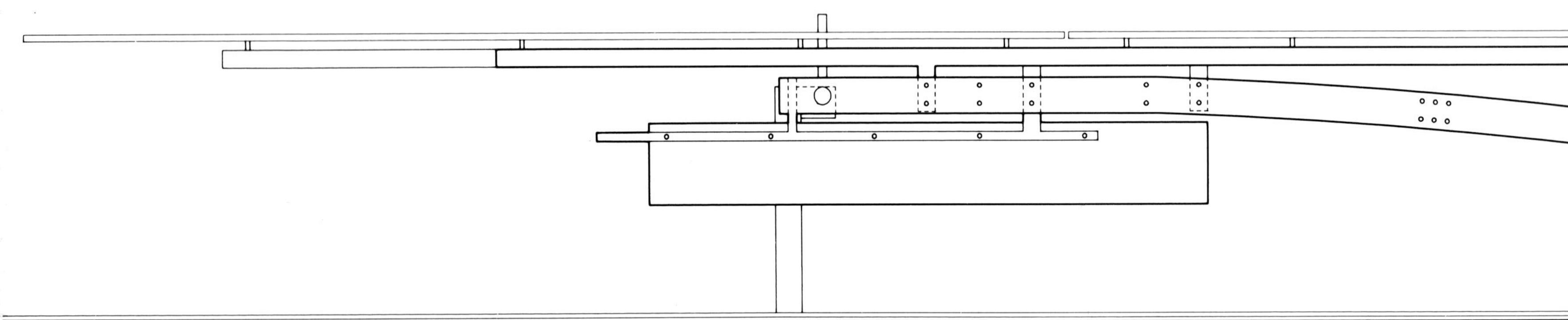

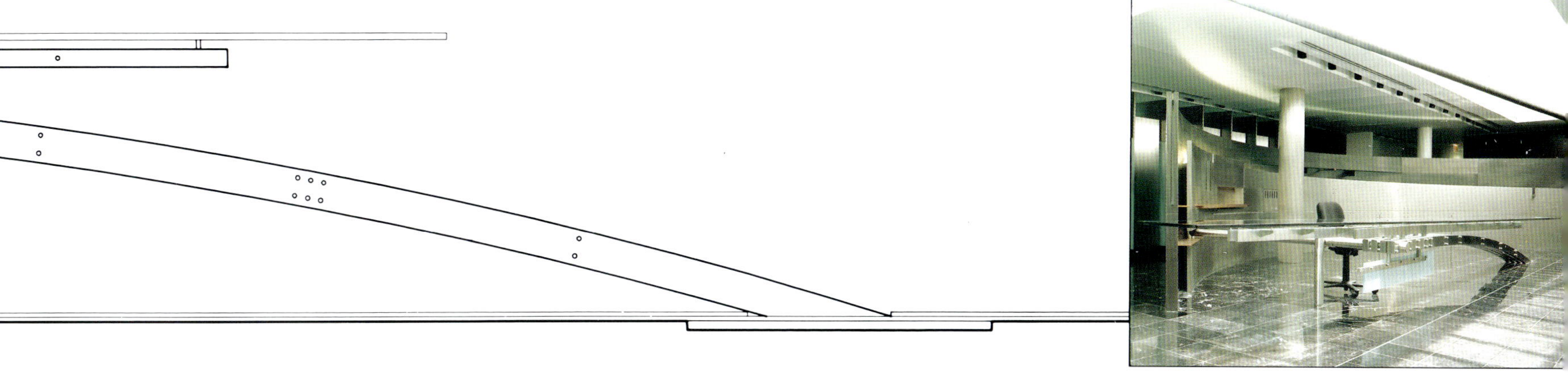

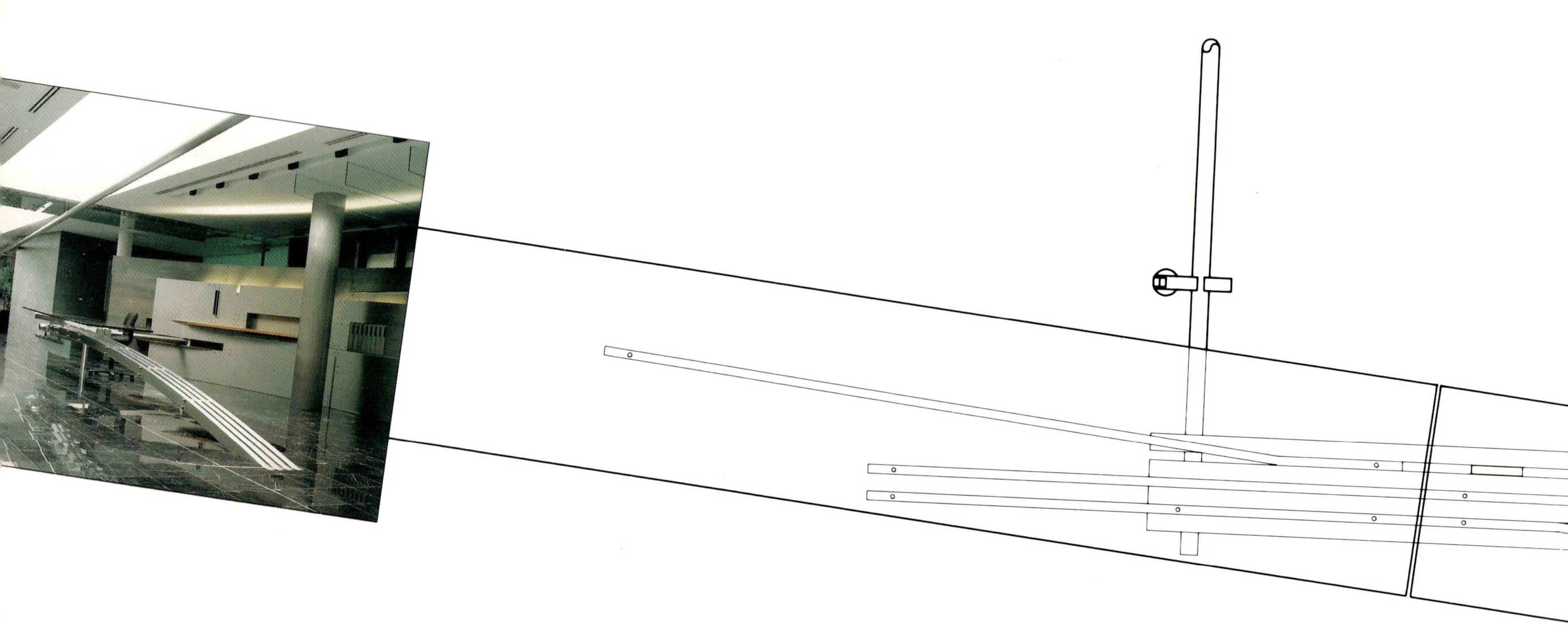

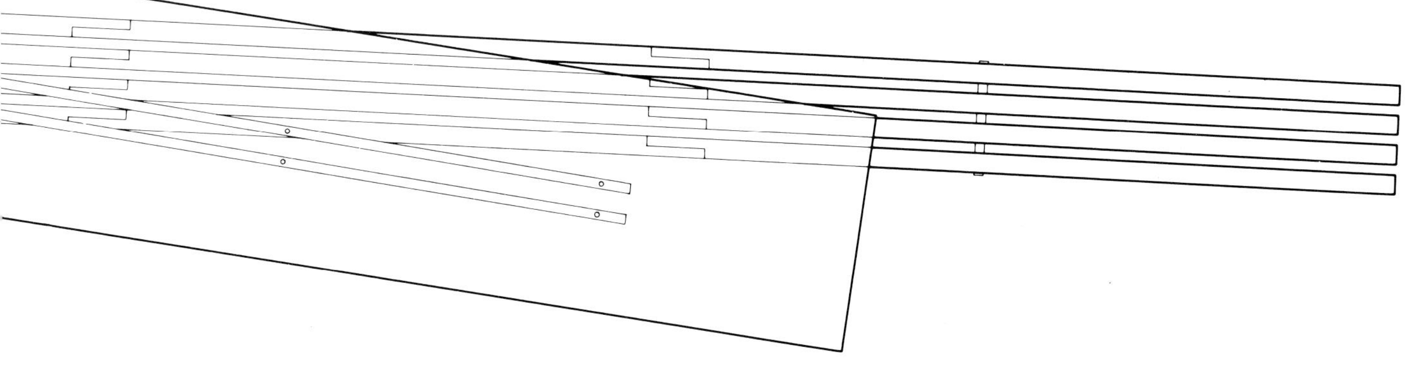

CANADIAN NATIONAL ROYAL TRUST OFFICE BUILDING COMPLEX

Toronto, Ontario, Canada, 1989

This is the first prize winner in the architectural competition, summer 1989. The overall urban approach is to design an authentic, contemporary modern building complex of the highest quality that relates to an area where all the existing buildings are modern; that defines the streets and relates creatively to the neighbouring SkyDome, CN Tower and office buildings; and sets forward a major architectural approach that will also be a guide and inspiration for the development of the adjacent open areas.

Both 20-storey office buildings – the Royal Trust Building at the corner of Front Street and Peter Street and the CN Office Building at the corner of Front Street and Spadina – are layered as 45-feet-wide wall buildings, giving each side of the complex a special character that relates to its streets and setting. In the Royal Trust mid-rise, the building wing along Front Street is placed parallel to the street, thereby connecting up with a series of existing buildings, all the way back to the railroad station. It is a pure, straight rectangular shape clad in black granite and glass. The other wing is gently curved – in a light green, all-glass curtain wall skin, giving it a lively movement and making a poetic gesture towards the SkyDome and other existing buildings.

The CN Building is tilted gently in plan to define the car and pedestrian movement to and from Spadina and Front Streets. The tilted glass and metal facade facing Front Street is also tilted vertically out towards the sidewalk, further articulating this important street intersection. The building wing facing the railroad tracks continues the movement of the curved Royal Trust building wing, and is also clad in an all-glass curtain wall. The articulation of building wings moves the project away from the conventional fat, deep office box buildings. From the interior, all staff, in the European tradition of shallow office buildings, will have exterior views and an abundance of light in their offices. In addition, many corner offices are provided.

Client: *CN Real Estate: Douglas Tipple, President; David Levin, Vice President; Michael Whelan, Senior Director, Development; Roger Petersen, Senior Director; Vicky Gordon, Development Manager*

Design Consultant Architects: *Ellerbe Becket, New York: Peter Pran, Design Principal; Carlos Zapata, Associate Design Director; Jill Lerner, Project Director; Lyn Rice, Project Architect; Ed Calma, Maria Wilthew, Curtis Wagner, Project Designers; Paul Davis; Jeff Walden; Tom Klose; Deborah Stiefel; Athene Carras, AES; Timothy Arnold; Vatche Aslanian; Berj Malikian, Designer; Frank Yu, Designer; Timothy Johnson, Designer; Ellerbe Becket, Washington DC; Greg Powe, Project Director; Mark Molen, Project Architect*

Architect of Record: *Dunlop Farrow, Toronto: Peter Warren, Project Director and Partner; Doug Neville, Project Manager and Partner; David Morgan, Associate Partner; Alar Kongats, Associate Partner, Senior Designer; Christian Klemt, Project Designer; Robert Chang, Project Designer; Nada Bajie; George Bitsakakis*

Planning Consultants: *IBI Group*

Construction Managers: *Constructors Eastern Inc*

Consulting Structural Engineers: *MS Yolles + Partners Ltd*

Consulting Mechanical Engineers: *Smith + Andersen*

Consulting Electrical Engineers: *Mulvey + Banani International Inc*

Consulting Landscape Architects: *Ferris McCluskey Quilln & Associates*

Traffic Consultants: *B-A Consulting Group Ltd*

Elevator Consultants: *KJA Consultants, Inc*

Environmental Engineering Consultants: *Rowan, Williams, Davies & Irwin, Inc*

Modelmakers Ellerbe Becket: *Lyn Rice, Eduardo Calma, Curtis Wagner, Maria Wilthew, Frank Yu, Mark Molen, Berj Malikian*

Models: *Richard Tenguerian*

Photographer: *Dan Cornish*

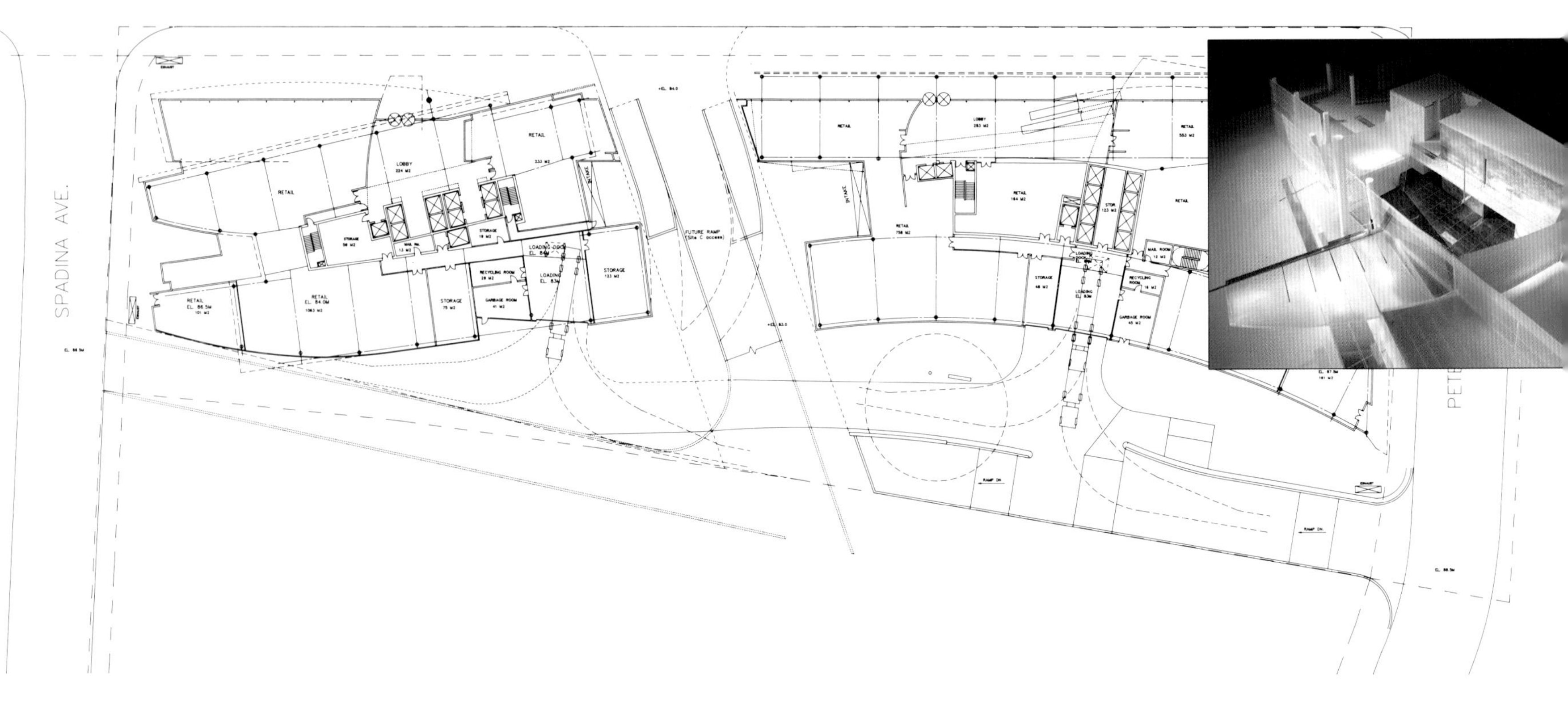

GROUND FLOOR PLAN

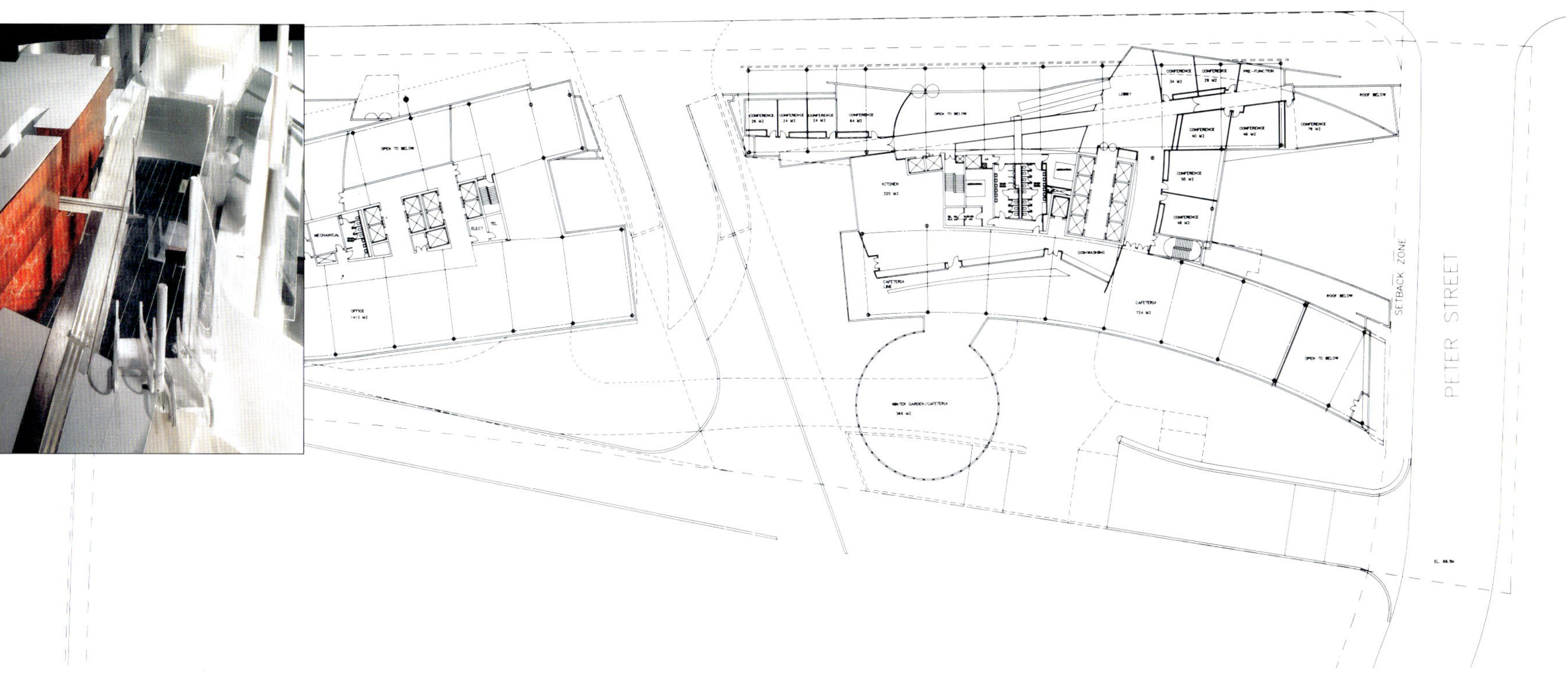

SECOND FLOOR PLAN

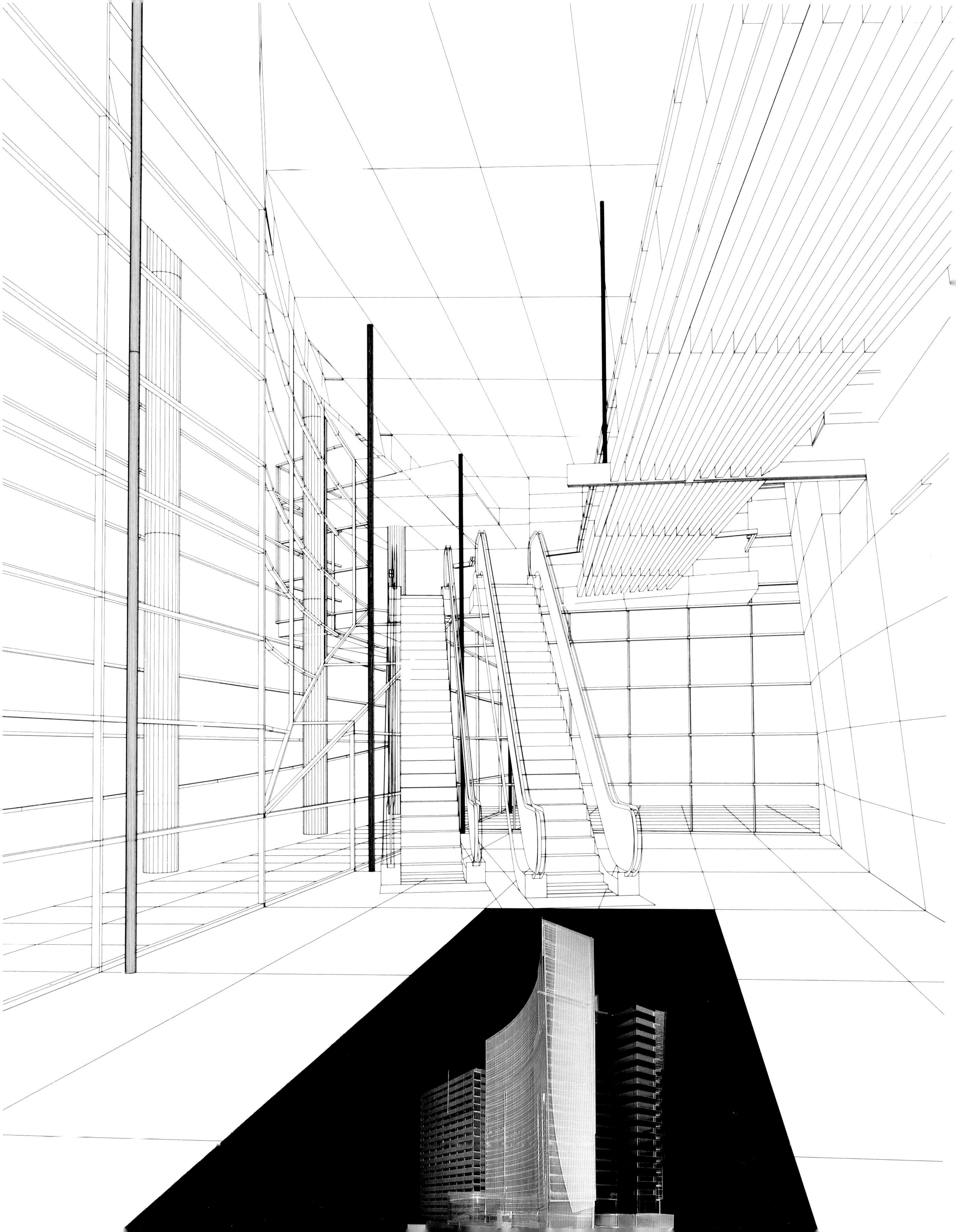

CANADIAN NATIONAL LABATTS HEADQUARTERS
Toronto, Ontario, Canada, 1990

The complex consists of a 20-storey office highrise, half of which will function as the Labatts Headquarters, a TV building for TSN studios and offices, a brewhall and beer museum for Labatts, and an apartment building with 254 units. The office building has a highly articulated plan and image, which has grown directly out of its site plan and close proximity to the SkyDome. The office highrise has a powerful and distinct shield shape ending the building towards the sky, giving it a unique character and recognisable image, locally, nationally and internationally. The executive offices on top of the building (behind the shield) have magnificent views towards the Toronto City Centre and into the SkyDome. The exterior skin of the office highrise is expressed in a layering of glass, metal and stone in a both rich and minimalist poetic articulation.

The beer hall along the Esplanade is given its main expression in the tilted oval, rising above its roof, which also provides for its main entry and exciting interior hall space, with its direction pointing towards the top of the Labatts Headquarters.

The TSN studio building has a sloping theatre-like roof, with curving walls tilting up towards the main public entrance along the street, celebrating the act of entry. The building shape expresses movement and excitement.

The highrise apartment building is articulated in two slabs: one straight and one with leaning walls. The internal plaza between the building units has a gentle slope up towards a view of the lake above the expressway. The ground floor of the highrise is comprised of retail and restaurant space. All the buildings are given distinction and character on each side of the complex, from the Gardener Expressway, the SkyDome, CN Tower, as well as from the rest of the city.

***Client**: CN Real Estate: Doug Tipple, President; Michael Whelan, Senior Director; David Levin, Vice President*
***Architects**: Ellerbe Becket Architects, New York Design Consultants: Peter Pran, Design Principal and Senior Vice President; Carlos Zapata, Senior Designer and Vice President; Eduardo Calma, Project Designer; Curtis Wagner, Project Designer; Berj Malikian, Designer; Maria Wilthew, Designer; Paul Davis, AES; Lyn Rice, Designer; Architect of Record: Dunlop Farrow: Peter Warren, Partner, Project Director; Mike Moxam, Associate Partner, Project Architect; Robert Chang, Designer, Model; Alar Kongat, Associate Partner, Designer*
***Small-Scale Model**: Tenguerian Models*
***Photographer**: Dan Cornish*

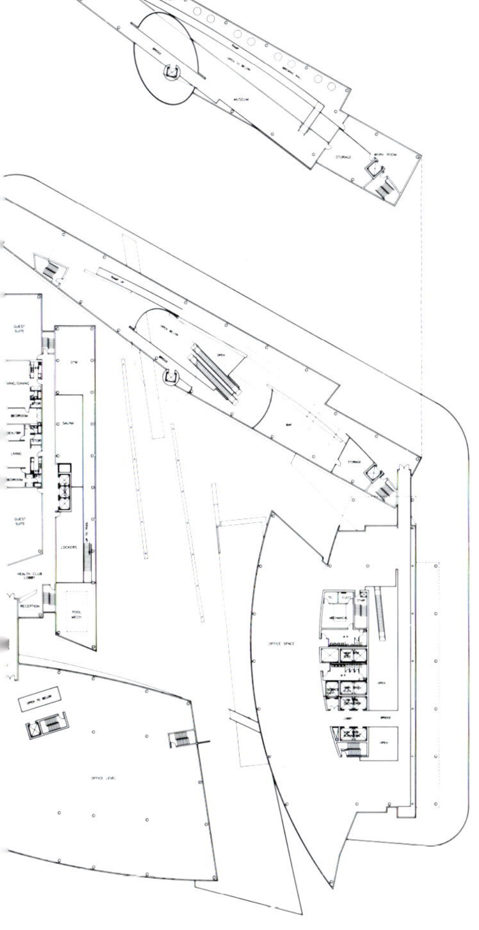

SECOND AND THIRD FLOOR PLANS

McCORMICK PLACE EXPANSION, STADIUM AND CONVENTION CENTER ADDITION
Chicago, Illinois, USA, 1990

The stadium has a 72,000 seating capacity and was proposed in conjunction with the new McCormick Place Expansion which has an exhibition area of over 850,000 square feet. An enclosed concourse ties together the two existing McCormick Place exhibition halls with the new one. A curved, raised enclosed walkway was proposed to link the McCormick Place Expansion and the Stadium.

The Stadium is tilted seven degrees in plan, to tie in with the new McCormick Place entry. A plaza in between the two major structures further emphasises this overall master plan, giving unity and dialogue between buildings. The Stadium has four major entries (north, south, east, west). The lower building wing to the north is placed parallel with Cermack Road to tie in with the general Chicago grid. That entry and the entry to the east facing the McCormick Place are considered the two major entries; however, the entry from Michigan to the west and the entry from the parking place to the south are also important. The dynamic overall asymmetrical composition of the Stadium responds to the specific functional requirements and the asymmetrical contextual setting (to the different sides).

The new McCormick Place Expansion has a building block of meeting rooms to the north between the exposition hall, the Galleria, and the truck and crate storage to the south of the exposition hall. A gently curved metal roof gives tremendous strength and image to the new building with its movement, glass opening and terrace towards Lake Michigan.

The overall design of the proposed multi-purpose domed Stadium and the McCormick Place Expansion is in the tradition and spirit of Chicago's best modern architecture and breaks new ground in today's leading modern architecture.

Early Study for a multi-purpose Domed Stadium and Convention Center Expansion (not to be built), Spring 1990, by Mc3D, Inc for Chicago's Metropolitan Pier and Exposition Authority

Developer: Stein & Company: Richard Stein, President; Michael Szkatulski, Senior Vice President/Development
Architects: A Epstein & Sons International Inc, Ellerbe Becket/TVS & Associates; A Epstein & Sons International Inc: Mickey Kupperman; Ted Amberg; Tony Chaitin; Ellerbe Becket: Ellerbe Becket, Kansas City: Ron Turner, Director; Gordon Wood, Project Director and Planners; Bill Johnson, Design Principal; John Selby, Project Manager; Tony Rohr, Project Architect; Ellerbe Becket, New York: Peter Pran, Design Principal; Carlos Zapata, Associate Design Director; Eduardo Calma, Project Designer; Curtis Wagner, Project Designer; Berj Malikian, Designer; Lyn Rice, Designer; Maria Wilthew, Designer; Tim Arnold, Designer; Ellerbe Becket, Minneapolis: Jon Sorenson, Project Architect; TVS & Associates: Tom Ventulett, Design Principal, Partner; Andy McLean, Principal-in-Charge, Partner
Contractors: George Hyman Construction; Huber Hunt & Nichols; Diesel Joint Venture; Walsh Construction; Louis Jones Enterprises; Alex Munoz Contractors
Photographer: Dan Cornish

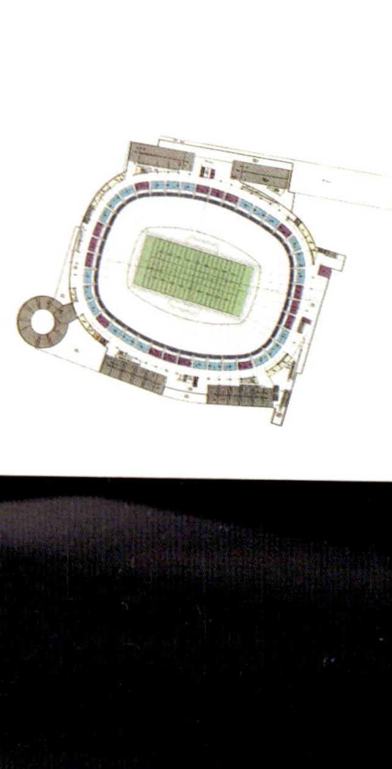 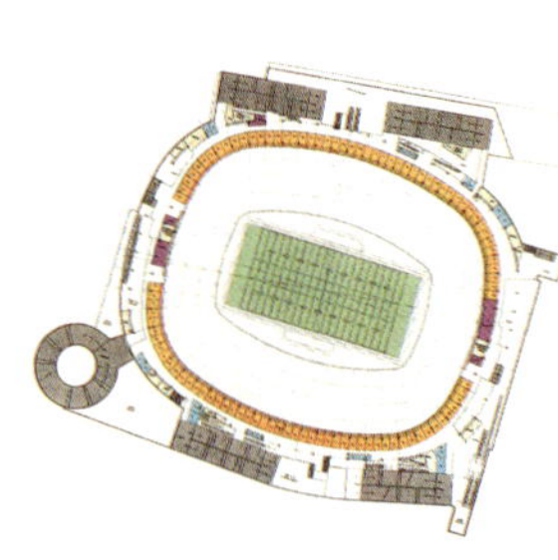  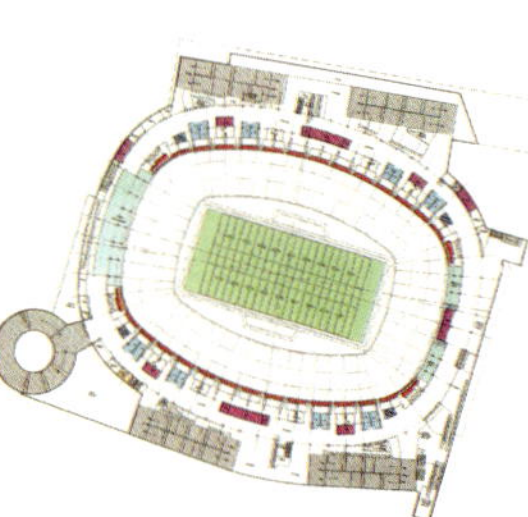 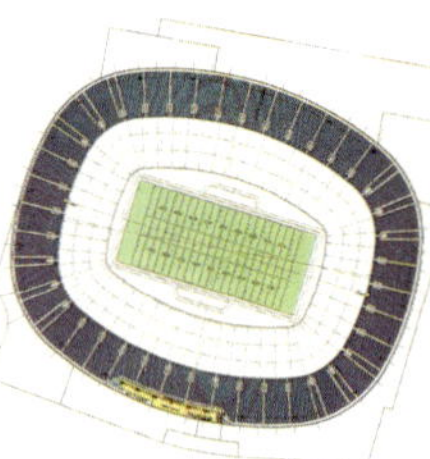

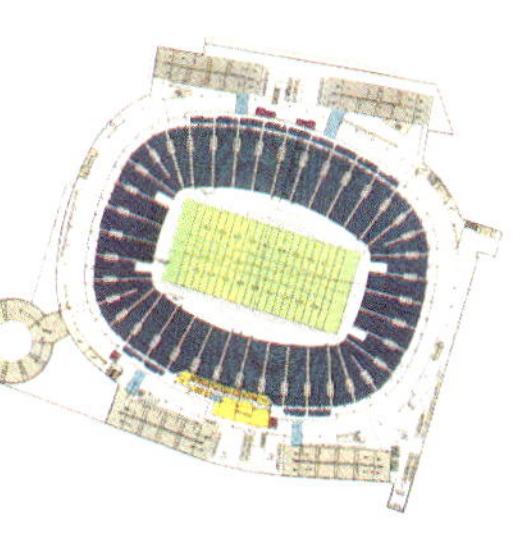 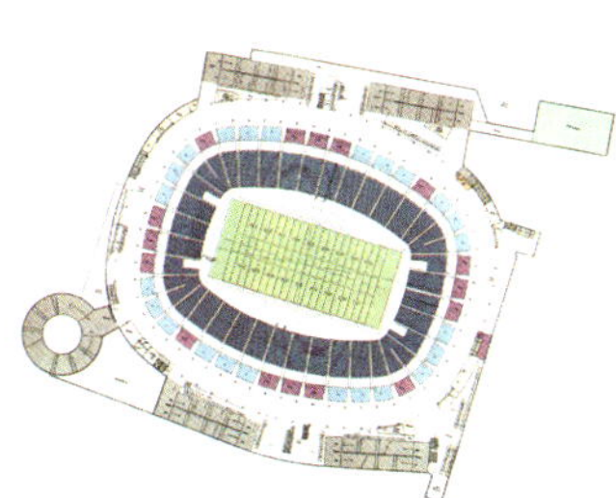 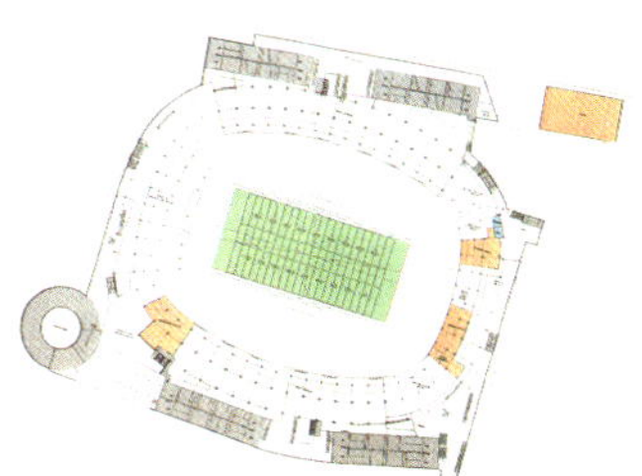 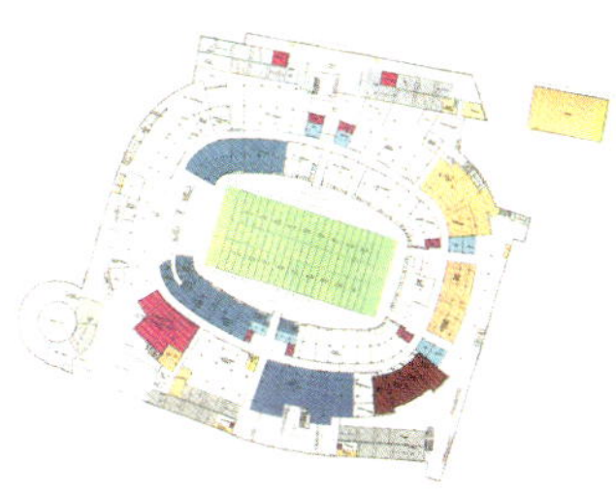

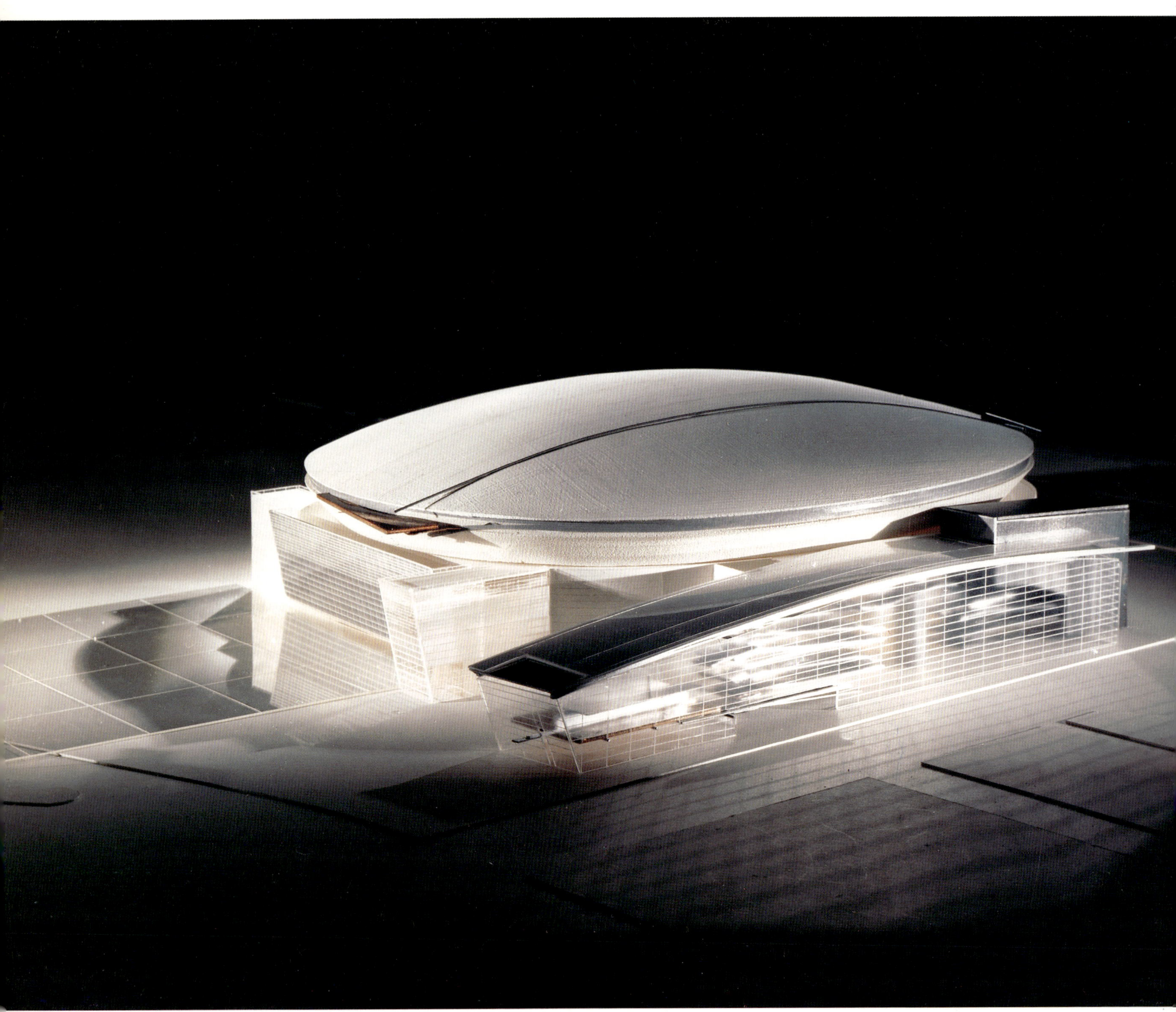

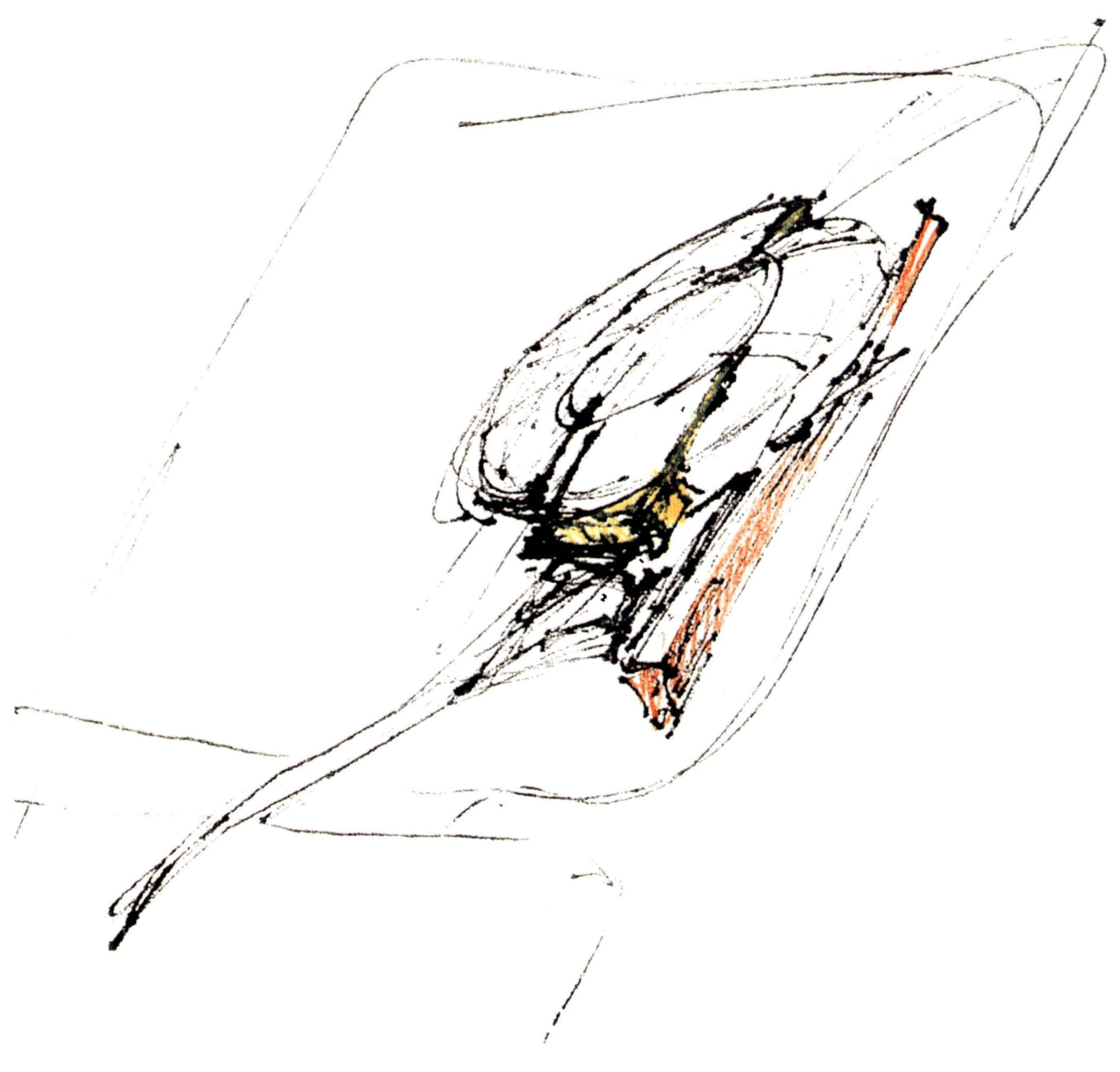

CONCEPT SKETCH FOR CHICAGO STADIUM

NEW RIKSHOSPITAL

Oslo, Norway, 1990

This project represents the hospital of the future, with the most advanced and progressive planning and design and a total construction cost of $350 million. The complex gently fits into the landscape and site setting and relates sensitively and creatively to the existing buildings. This solution allows for internal flexibility and external expansion for future needs. The overall plan has provided for an excellent separate out-patient and in-patient corridor/circulation system. A gently curved spine/atrium corridor space to the east is the backbone of the proposal.

In general, the second floor contains radiology and emergency, the third floor operating rooms and recovery, the fourth floor university/research functions and administration and the fifth floor the main cafeteria/restaurant with a spectacular view of the Oslofjord.

Daylight is provided for all rooms where staff work more than four hours per day ensuring a uniquely humane hospital.

Brovold, Peter Grandine, L Wilson Kidd, Mike Medina, Duane Ramseth, Jan Tasker, Aarin Ayad, Kelly Vandeplasse, Mike Hnastchenko, Medical Planners
Photographer: *Dan Cornish*

Client: *SBED, (The State's Building and Property Department) State of Norway: Kjell Johannessen; Bård Rane*
Architects: *Ellerbe Becket, New York and Minneapolis; Bergersen, Gromholt & Ottar, Oslo; Bjorn Wessel & Associates, Oslo; Gunnarsjoo & Kolstad, Oslo; Bo Castenfors, Stockholm Ellerbe Becket, New York and Minneapolis: Peter Pran, Design Principal; Carlos Zapata, Design Director; Eduardo Calma, Tim Johnson, Lyn Rice, Curtis Wagner, Maria Wilthew, Paul Davis, AES, Dave Koenen, AES, Project Designers; Jill Lerner, Ray Skorupa, Project Managers; Ray*

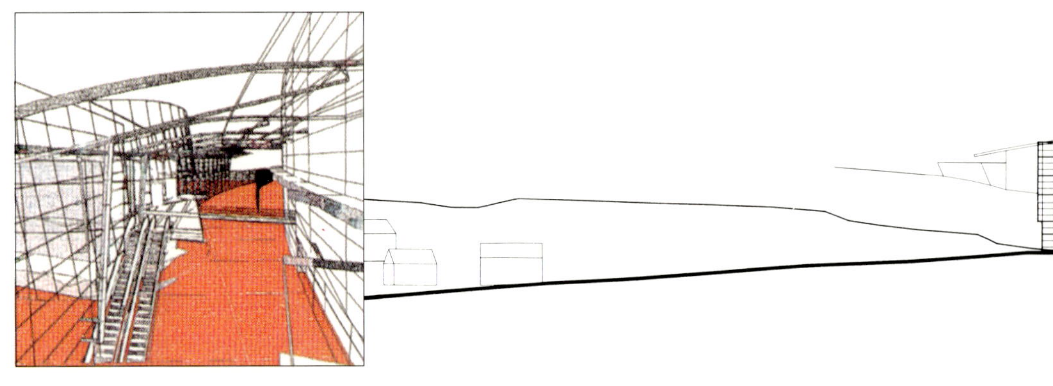

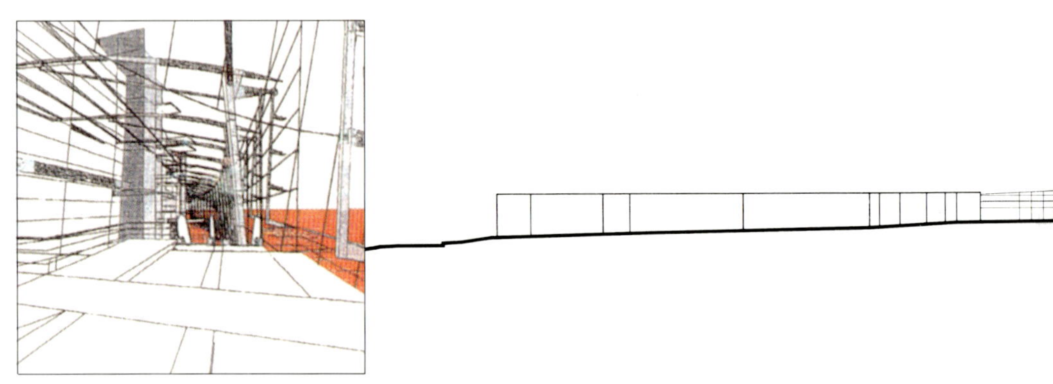

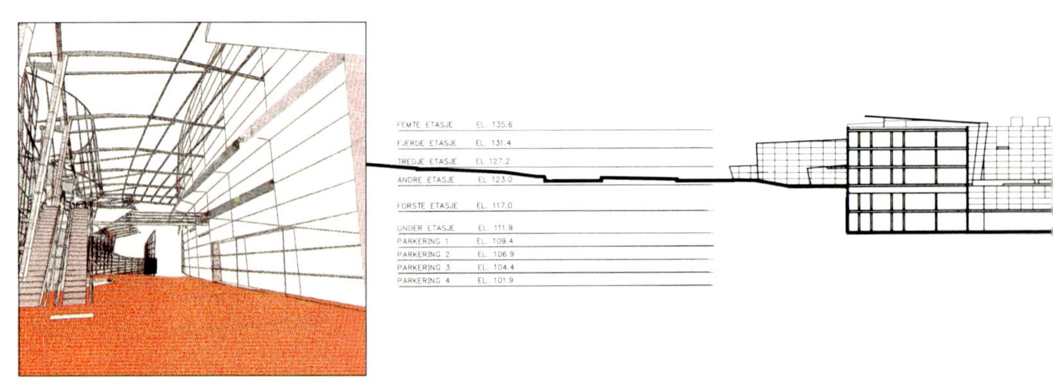

FEMTE ETASJE   EL. 135.6
FJERDE ETASJE   EL. 131.4
TREDJE ETASJE   EL. 127.2
ANDRE ETASJE   EL. 123.0
FORSTE ETASJE   EL. 117.0
UNDER ETASJE   EL. 111.9
PARKERING 1   EL. 109.4
PARKERING 2   EL. 106.9
PARKERING 3   EL. 104.4
PARKERING 4   EL. 101.9

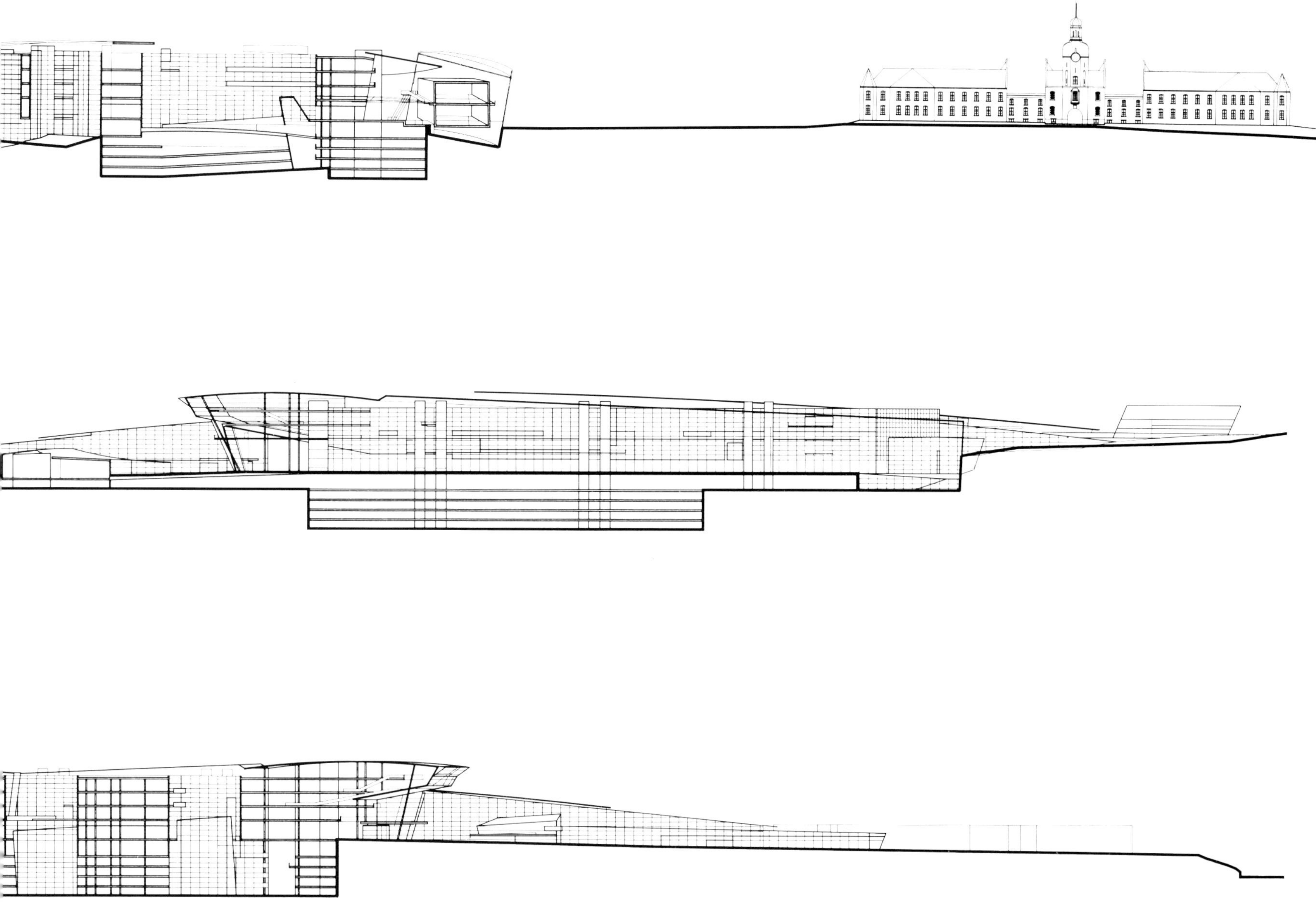

SITE PLAN

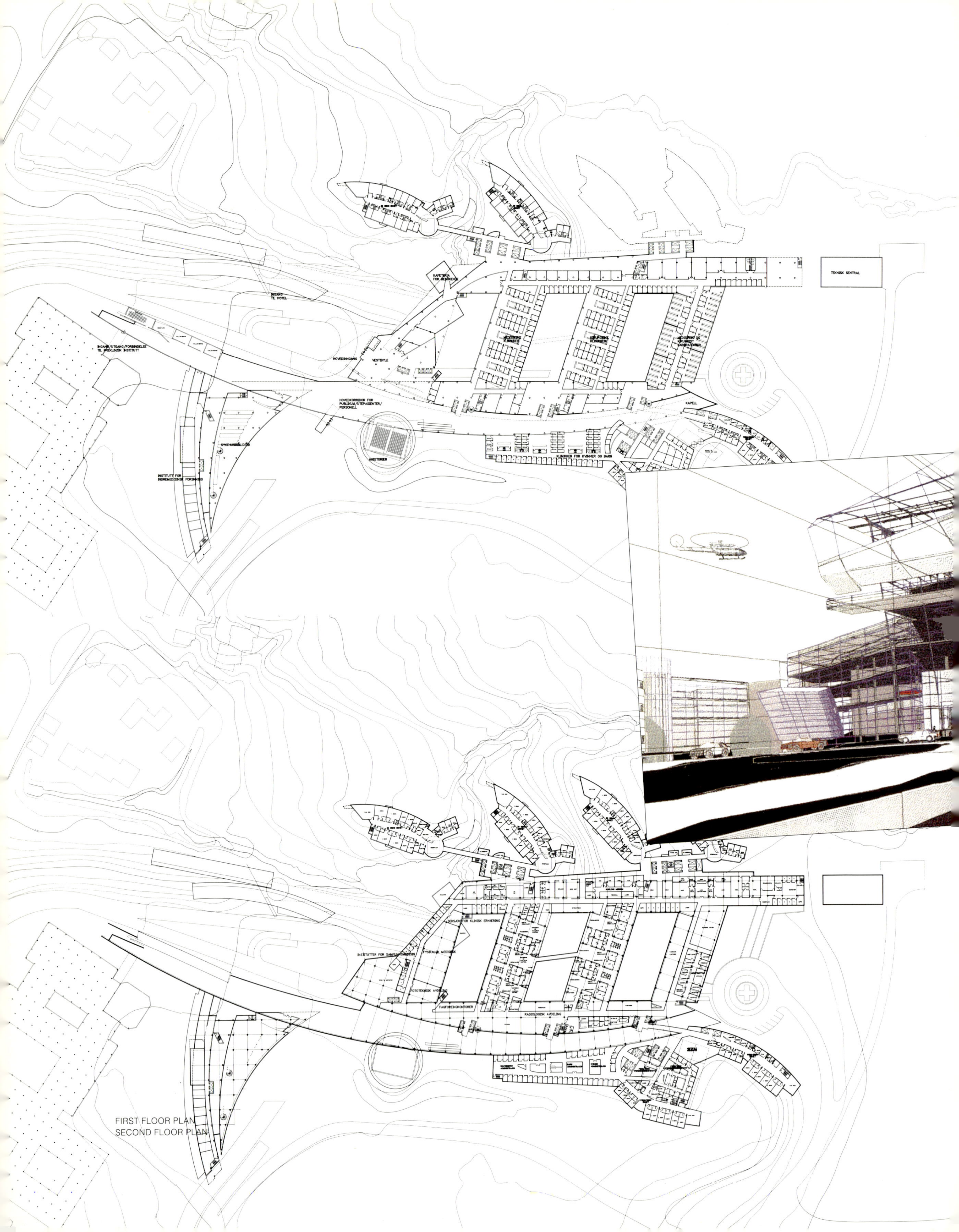

TEKNISK SENTRAL
KAFETERIA FOR BESØKENDE
INNGANG TIL HOTEL
INNGANG/UTGANG/FORBINDELSE TIL PREKLINISK INSTITUTT
HOVEDINNGANG
VESTIBYLE
SYKEHUSBIBLIOTEK
INSTITUTT FOR INDREMEDISINSK FORSKNING
HOVEDKORRIDOR FOR PUBLIKUM/STEFASENTER/PERSONELL
AUDITORIER
KAPELL
KLINIKKER FOR KVINNER OG BARN
INSTITUTTER FOR SAMFUNNSMEDISIN
SEKSJON FOR KLINISK ERNÆRING
FYSIKALSK MEDISIN
FOTOTEKNISK AVDELING
FAGFORENINGSKONTORER
RADIOLOGISK AVDELING
FIRST FLOOR PLAN
SECOND FLOOR PLAN

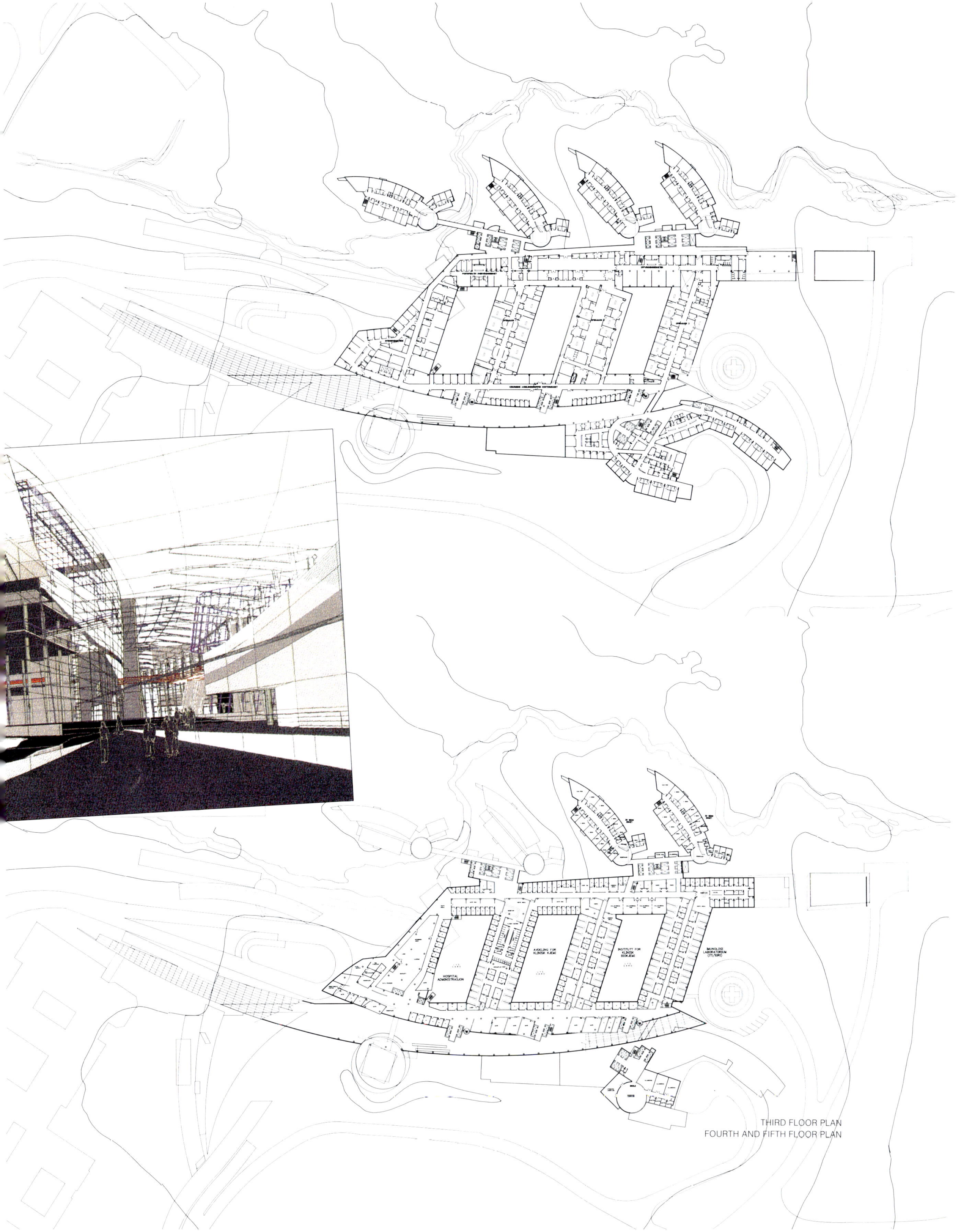

THIRD FLOOR PLAN
FOURTH AND FIFTH FLOOR PLAN

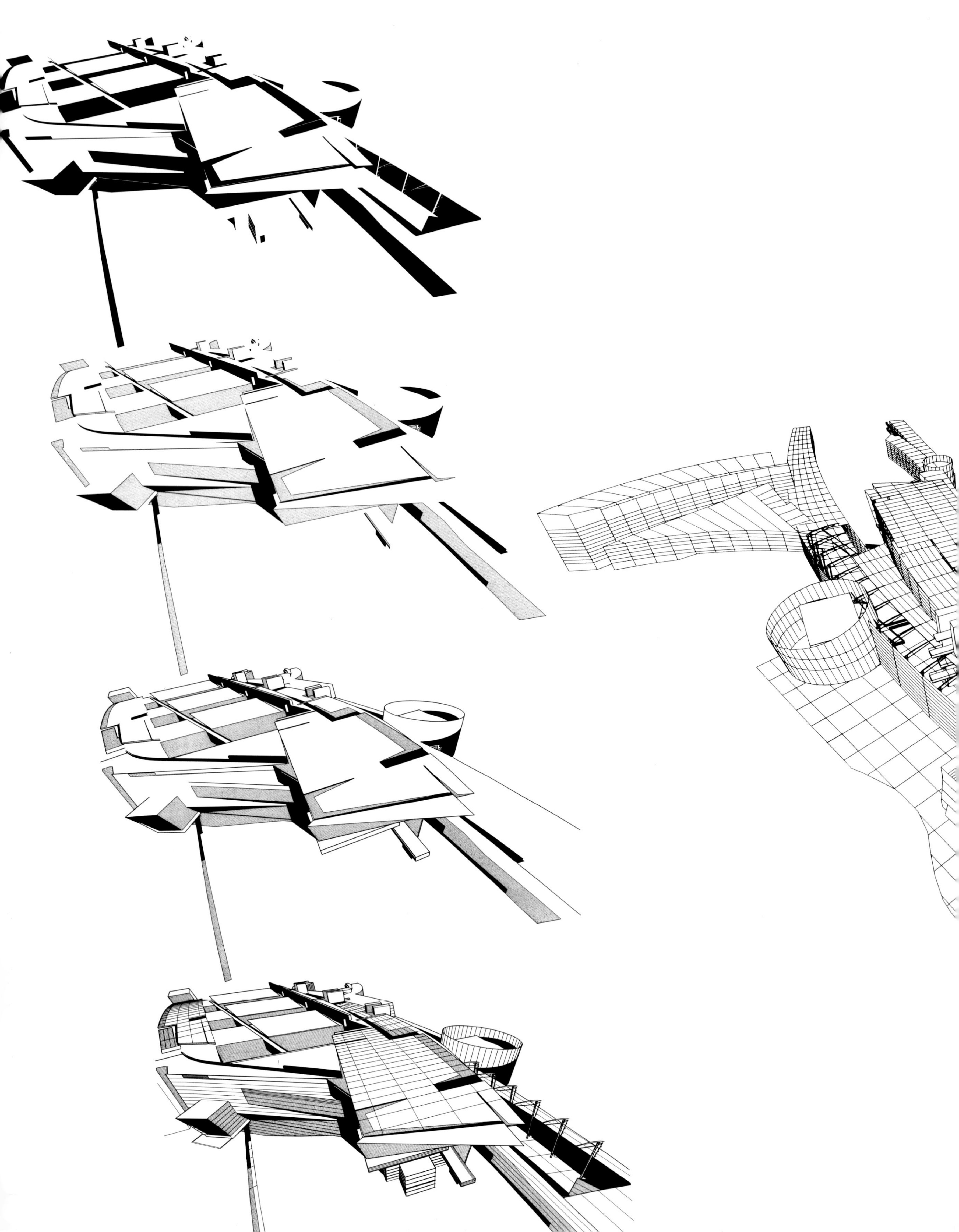

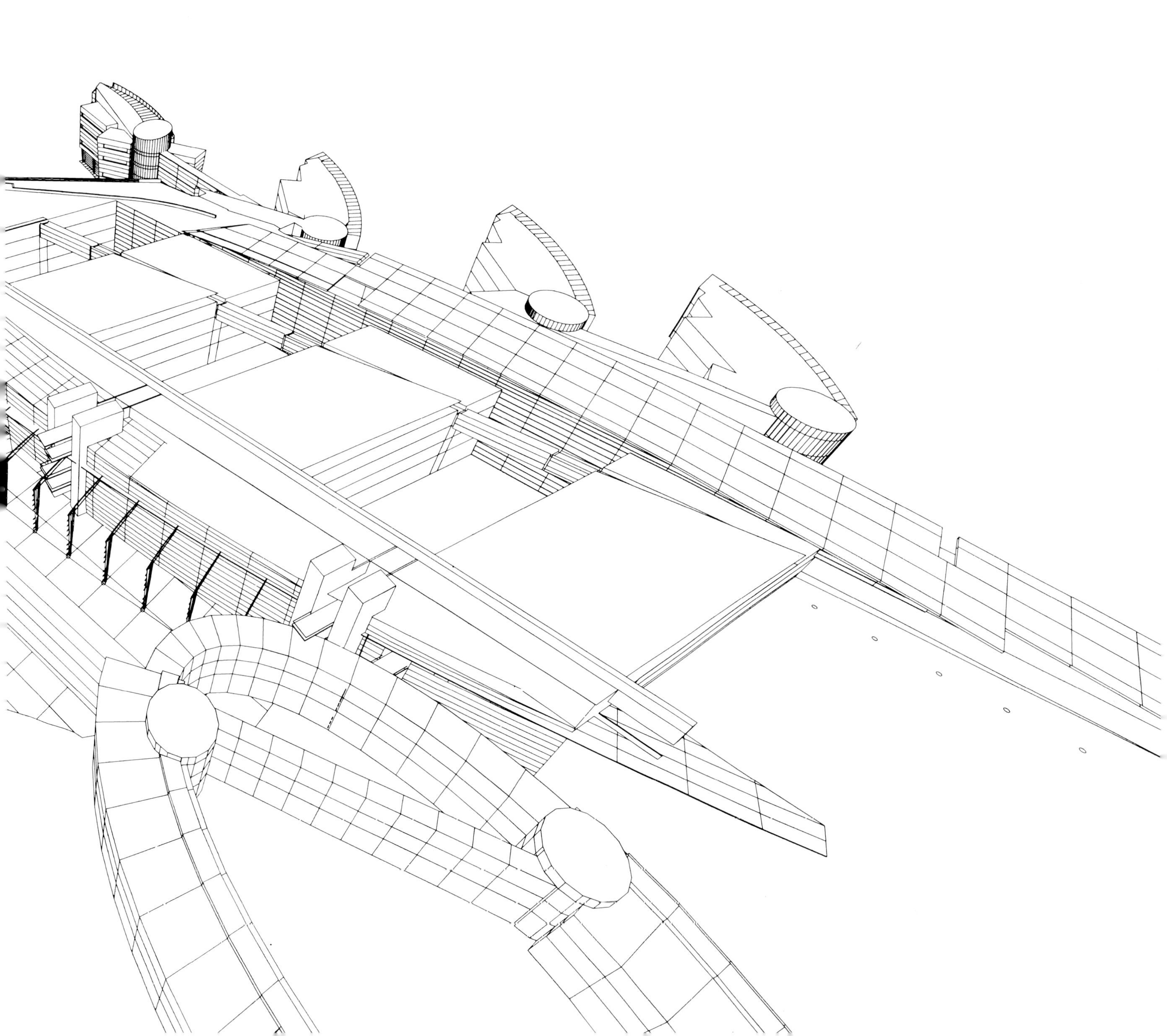

BANCO POPULAR DEL ECUADOR
Quito, Ecuador, 1990

Simple but expressive, this design is a poetic response to the moving topography of the city of Quito. It is a small building of 3,500 square feet, designed in a manner that distinguishes it from its surroundings, the intuition of Banco Popular being to communicate its presence through architecture, not through signage. Its powerful flowing curved roof creates a unique character and a recognisable image.

The building is composed of two main elements, a curved stainless-steel roof oriented towards the intersection of Av 6 de Diciembre and Av Portugal (main entry point) and a low curved glass element (parallel to Av 6 de Diciembre) which ties the building back to its immediate setting. The curved roof houses the banking hall while the low glass element contains the support spaces: staff cafeteria, storage, toilets, 24-hour cash machine, and stairs to the downstairs vault.

The building, located in a changing neighbourhood characterised by its diverse building types, is surrounded by a series of one-family houses to the north and west, a public high school and movie theatre to the south, a one-storey bank branch to the east, and 20-storey residential towers to the north-east.

__Client__: Banco Popular del Ecuador: Nicolas Landes, Executive President; Catalina Landes, Architectural Advisor
__Architect__: Ellerbe Becket, New York: Carlos Zapata, Vice President and Design Director; Potor Pran, Design Principal and Senior Vice President; Eduardo Calma, Project Designer;

Curtis Wagner, Project Designer; Maria Wilthew, Project Designer; Paul Davis, Designer; Lyn Rice, Designer; Timothy Johnson, Designer; Helen Ferguson, Designer; Melissa Koff, Coordinator
__Photographers__: Dan Cornish, Maria Curran

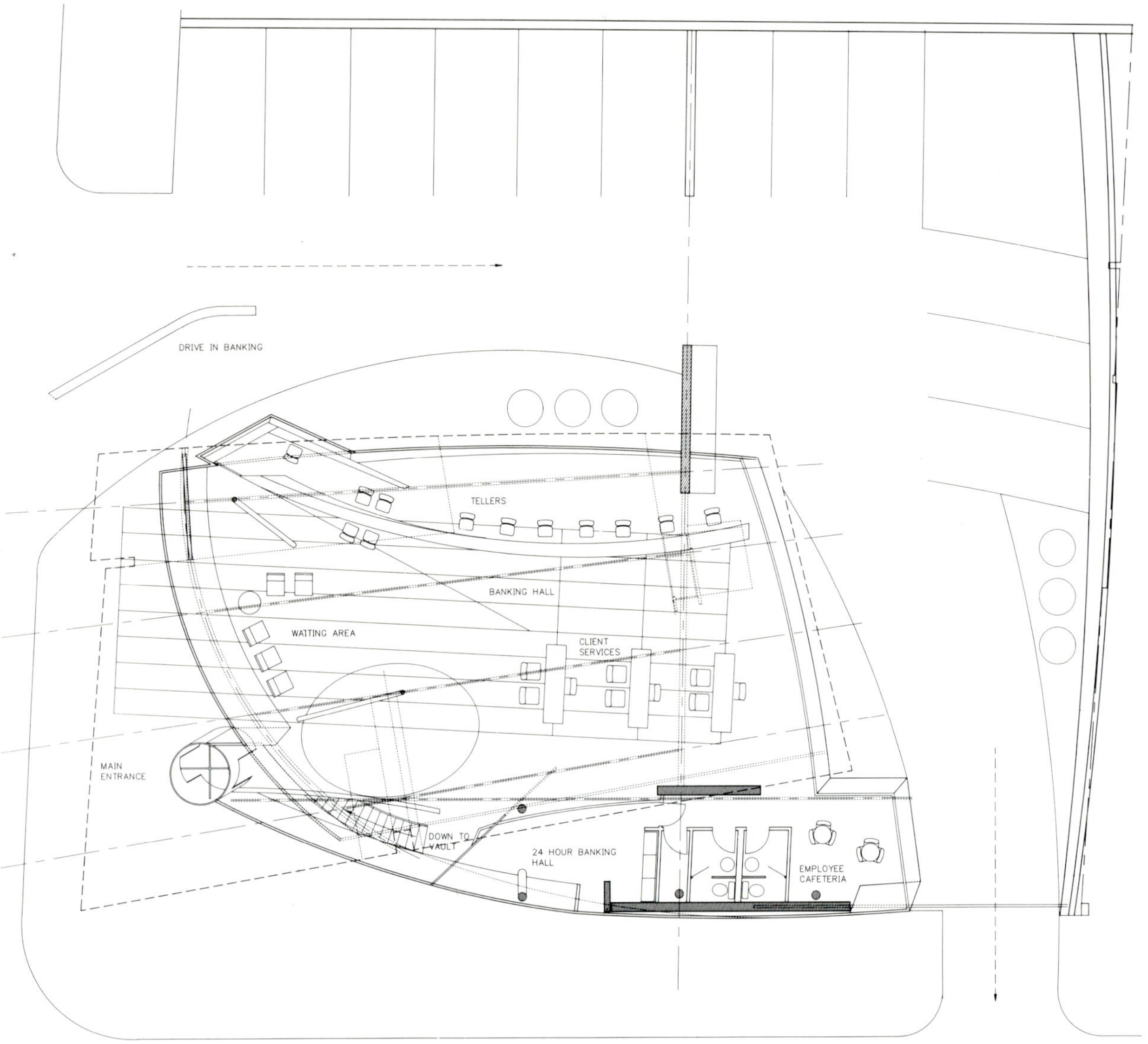

MAIN FLOOR PLAN

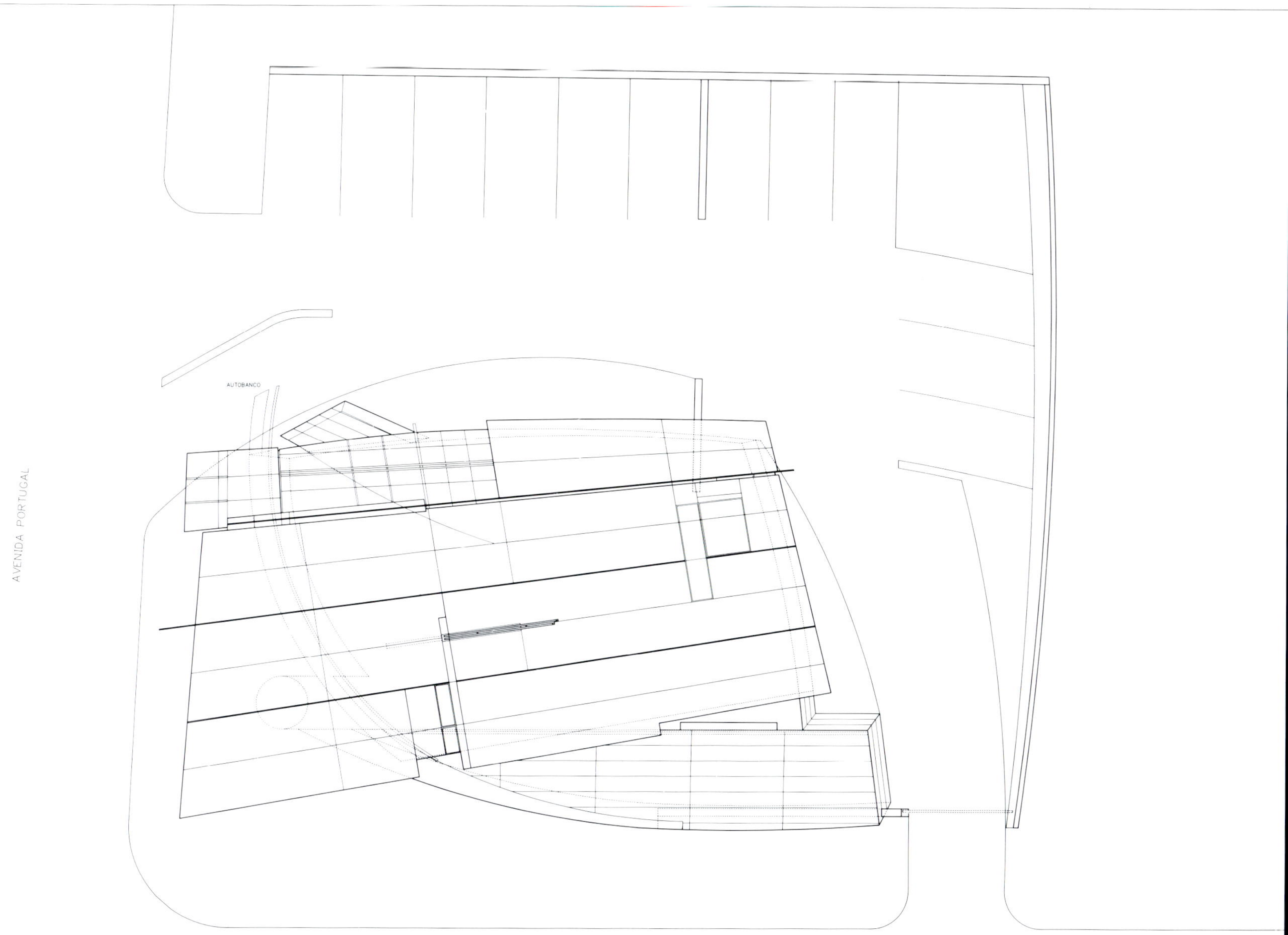

ROOF PLAN

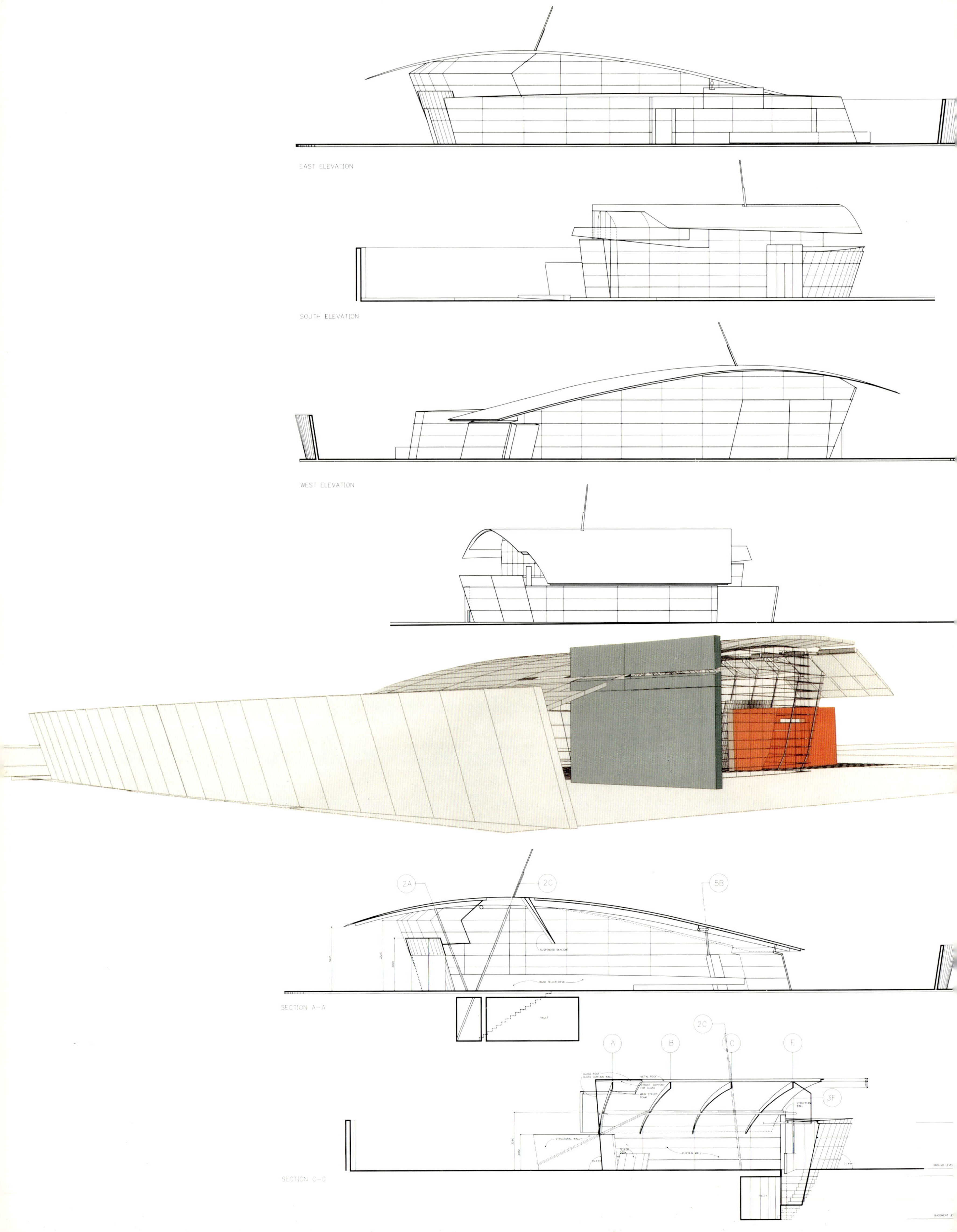

EAST ELEVATION

SOUTH ELEVATION

WEST ELEVATION

SECTION A-A

SECTION C-C

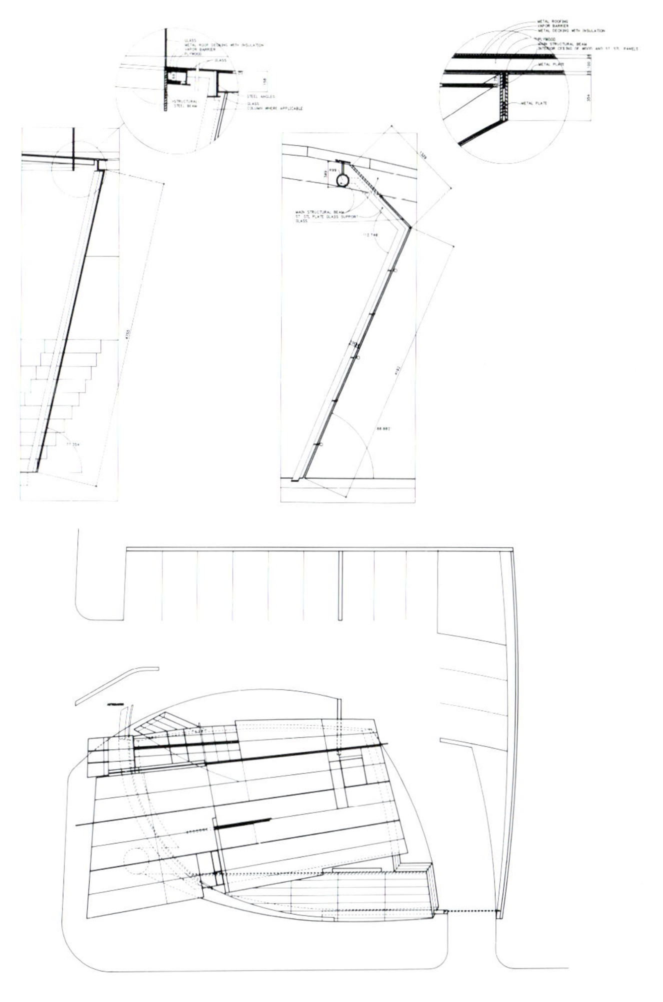

DETAIL OF ROOF/BEAM
CONNECTION

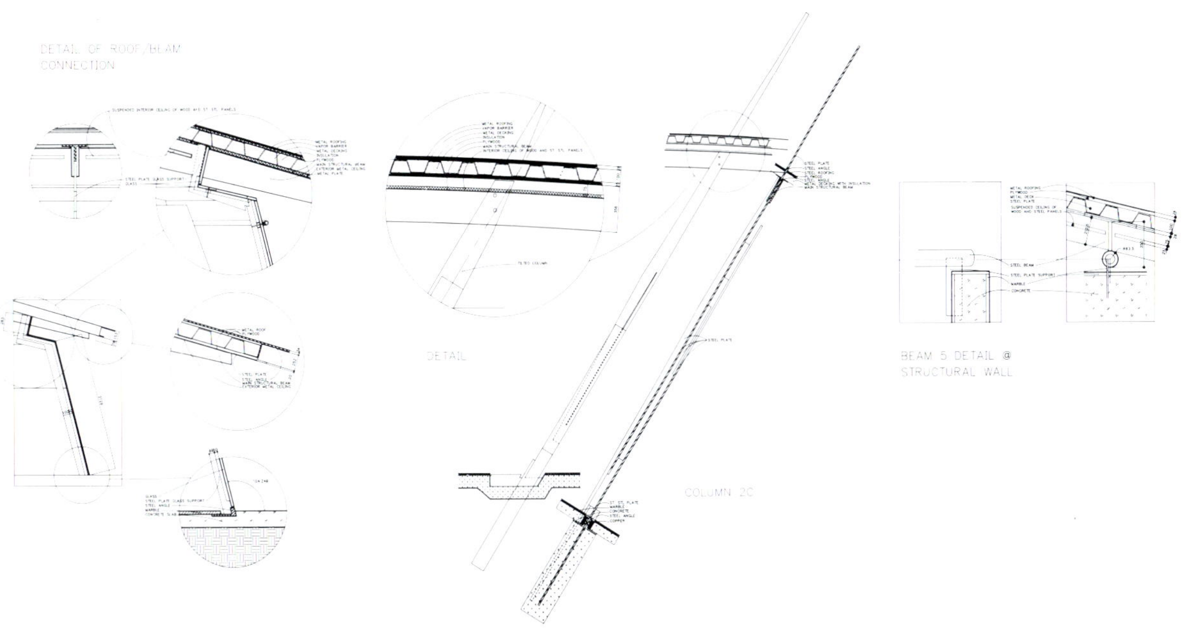

DETAIL

COLUMN 20

BEAM 5 DETAIL @
STRUCTURAL WALL

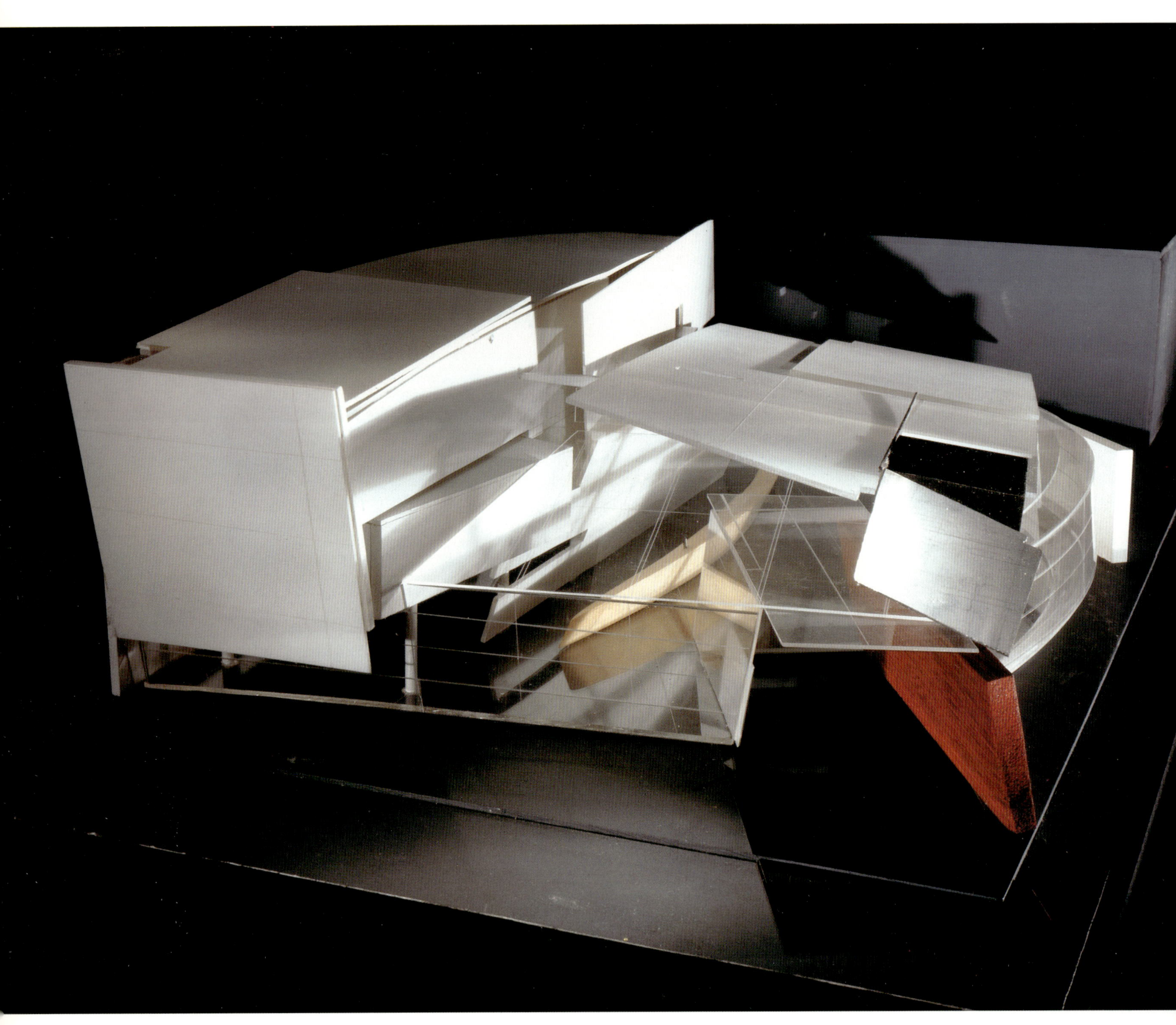

BANCO POPULAR DEL ECUADOR
Ibarra, Ecuador, 1991

This is the second of a series of prototype studies for Banco Popular del Ecuador. This new 9,500 square foot building derives its massing, scale and colour scheme directly from the existing site elements. The colour (white) responds to a city zoning regulation. The two-storey office wing reflects and continues the height of the neighbouring two-storey building immediately to the east, while the straight, tilted roof structure of the banking hall continues the one-storey expression characteristic of the south side of Olmedo Street.

The two-storey office structure and the tilted floating roof are delicately juxtaposed with the intention of creating a clear and welcoming gesture providing an open banking hall full of natural light and visually accessible to the neighbourhood.

Client: Banco Popular del Ecuador:
Nicolas Landes, Executive President;
Catalina Landes, Architectural Advisor
Architects: Ellerbe Becket,
Design Team: Carlos Zapata, Design
Director; Peter Pran, Design Principal;
Eduardo Calma, Project Designer;
Curtis Wagner, Project Designer;
Timothy Johnson, Project Designer
Photographers: Dan Cornish,
Maria Curran

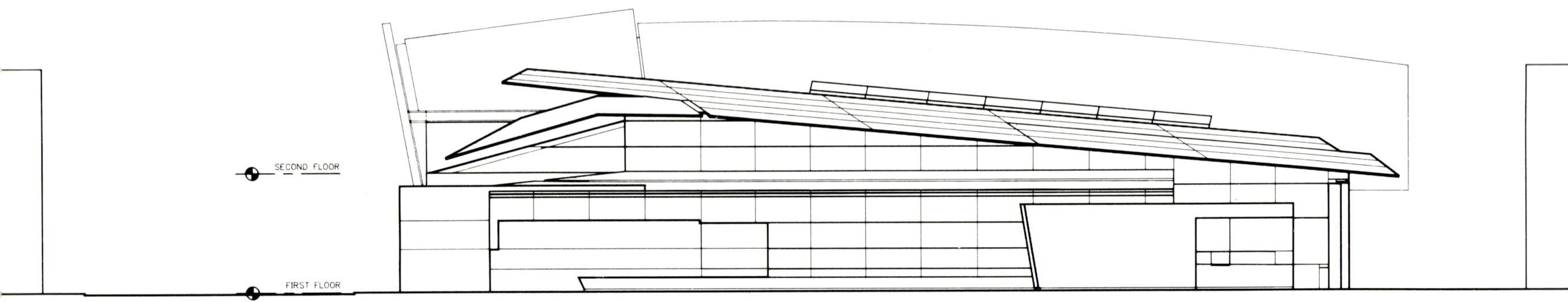

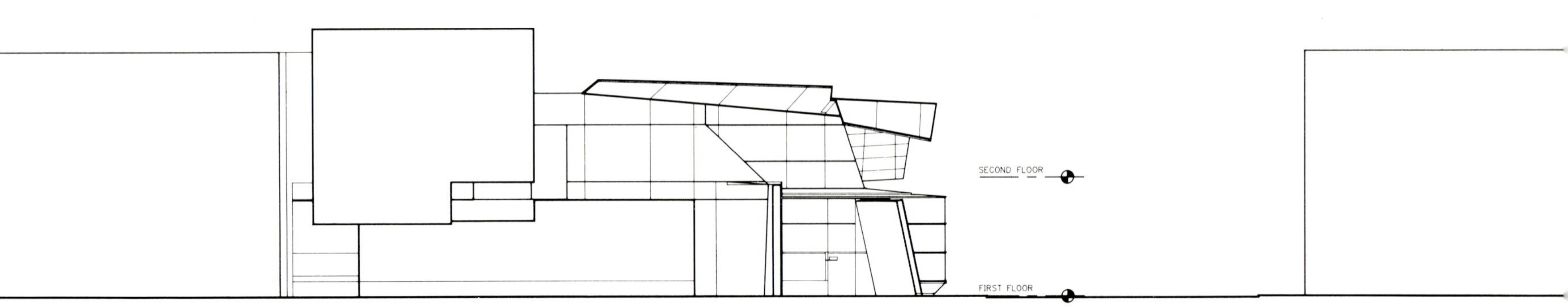

WEST ELEVATION
NORTH ELEVATION

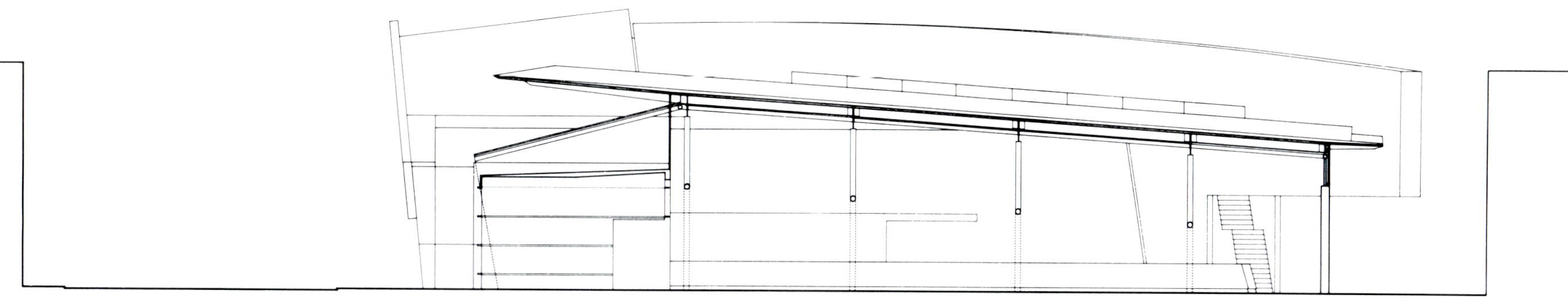

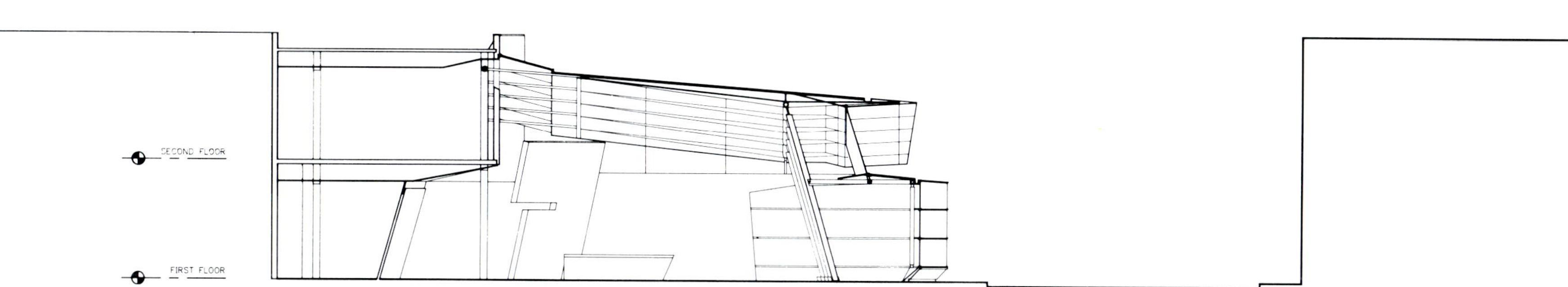

LONGITUDINAL SECTION
CROSS SECTION

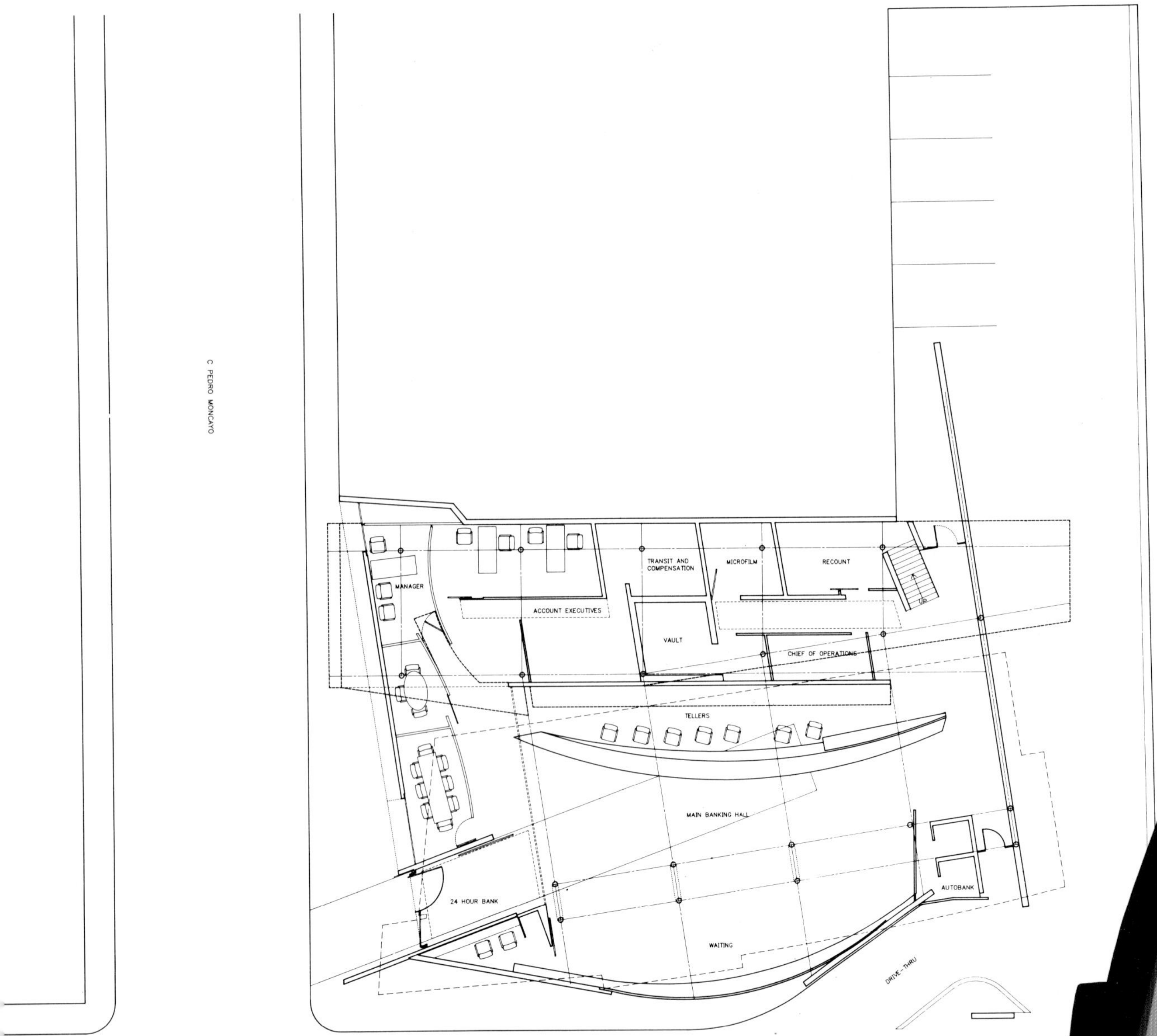

C PEDRO MONCAYO
MANAGER
ACCOUNT EXECUTIVES
TRANSIT AND COMPENSATION
MICROFILM
RECOUNT
VAULT
CHIEF OF OPERATIONS
TELLERS
MAIN BANKING HALL
24 HOUR BANK
AUTOBANK
WAITING
DRIVE-THRU
FIRST FLOOR PLAN

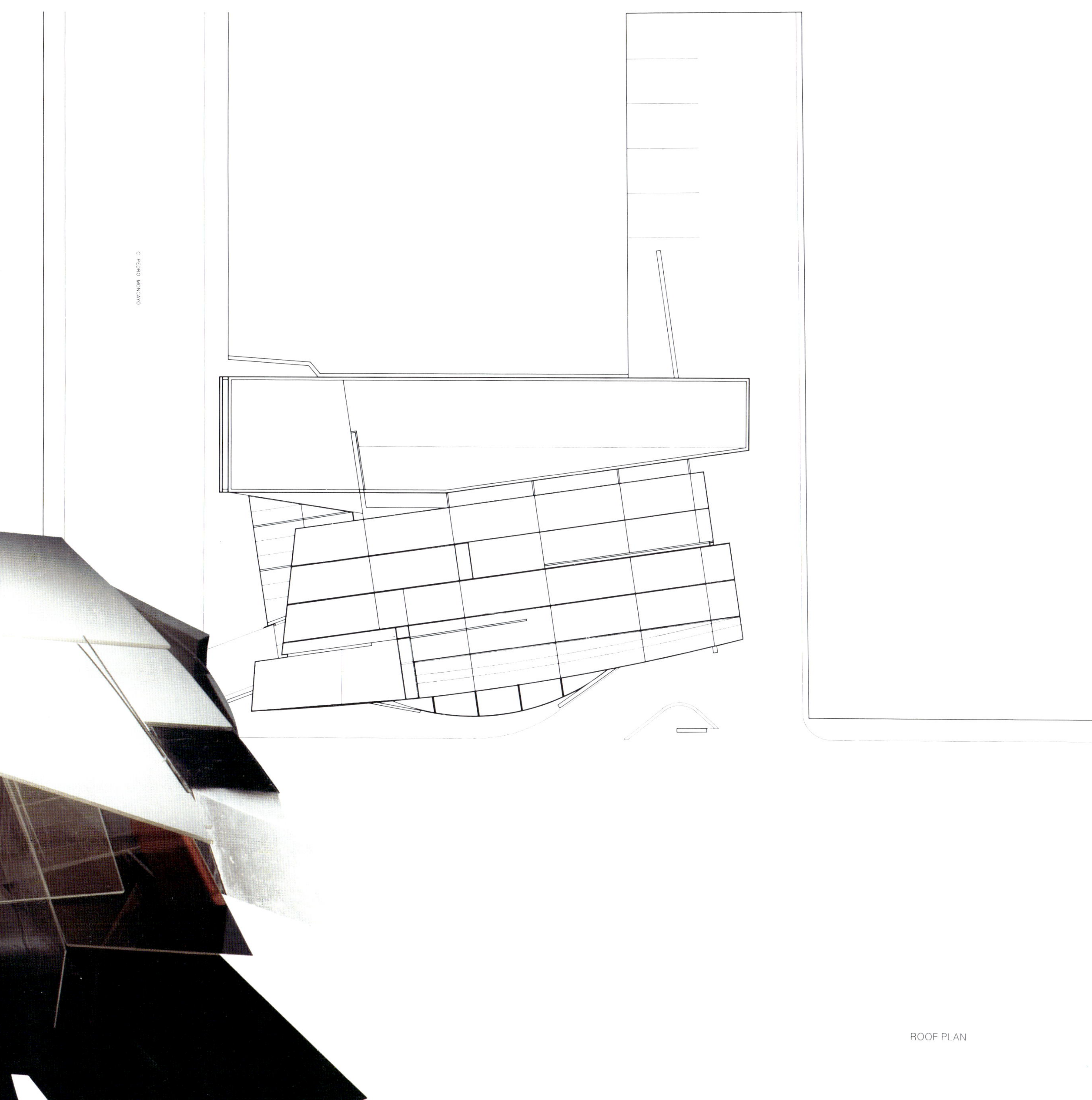
ROOF PLAN

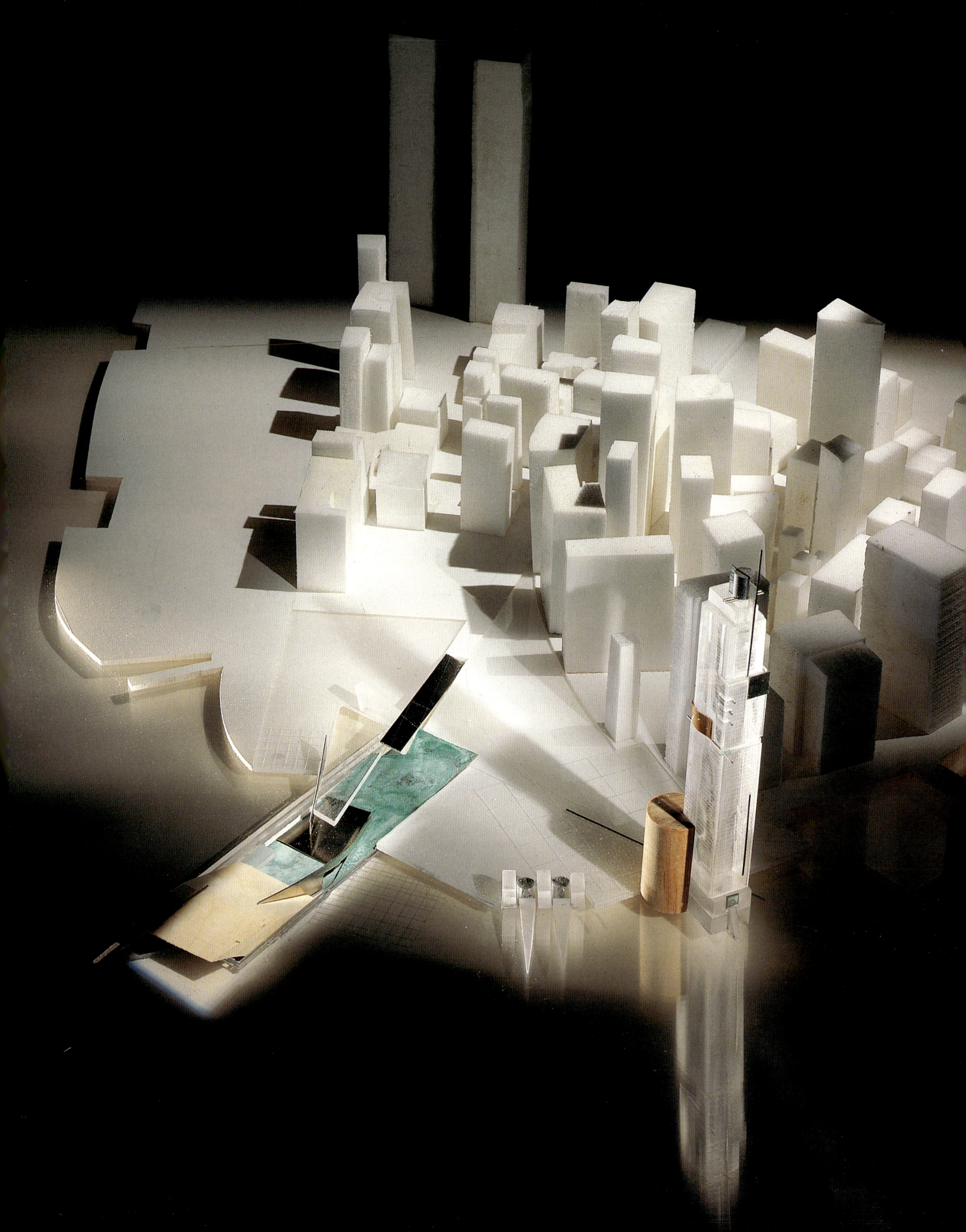

MANHATTAN SOUTH DEVELOPMENT

New York, USA, 1991

An into-the-water sunken public space, an extrusion to Battery Park and a flight from the verticality of the city, this is a further development and complement to our South Ferry project.

The sunken plaza and gardens extend into the water, and their overall shape and direction can be seen as an extension and endpoint to Broadway. A portion of Battery Park green space is tilted gently into the sunken space, which has an outdoor concert amphitheatre, seating areas, outdoor cafes, children's playground and a sound insulated subway tunnel exposed in glass and metal which floats in the air. The southern end of the sunken space has an indoor restaurant, tilting gently upwards above the sea line giving a magnificient view of the New York City waterfront.

The model photo shows the two projects combined into one coherent statement.

Architects: *Ellerbe Becket: Carlos Zapata, Design Director; Peter Pran, Design Principal; Timothy Johnson, Project Designer; Curtis Wagner, Project Designer; Helen Ferguson, Designer*
Photographer: *Dan Cornish*

RESORT HOTEL
Okinawa, Japan, 1991

A 400 room resort hotel on the coast, this is a commissioned project including three restaurants and major kitchen banquet rooms, health club, bar, disco and other facilities on the lower floors. The tilted, curved building creates a theatre-like exterior space to the water, where all the resort hotel activities take place. Every function has its own major shape and space. A four-storey glass-shaped atrium, that is piercing through the tilted curved hotel shape, contains the main entry and lobby. The typical hotel floor has a single-loaded corridor so that all the guest rooms have panoramic views.

Client*: name withheld*
Architects*: Ellerbe Becket, CCI Minneapolis and CCI New York: Richard Varda, Design Principal; Peter Pran, Design Principal; Gerald Simon, Project Director; Tim Johnson, Designer; Curtis Wagner, Designer*
Photographer*: Terry Wilkinson*

COLUMBIA UNIVERSITY RESEARCH CENTER
New York, USA, 1991

Placed at the major intersection of 168 Street and Broadway, where the diagonal street intersects with the octagonal city street grid, this 12-storey research centre creates a gentle dialogue and transfer in building mass between the 20-storey institutional Columbia Presbyterian Medical Centre along Broadway to the west and the continuous row of five-storey apartment buildings to the north, east and south.

The 300,000 square foot research centre is articulated in three building units, that together create a feeling of movement around an open atrium, to which three public entries lead. This creative urban approach forms a very friendly, rich, new building type in this northern part of Manhattan. The typical upper floor contains mostly wet labs for research with adjacent research offices and conference rooms. The ground floor contains staff and community oriented shops and restaurants. A second, rectangular scheme with a cube-shaped conference center at the top, provides a similarly appropriate and delightful solution.

The entire complex creates a new, progressive, invigorating and exciting architectural solution in one of the most important urban centres in New York City.

__Client__: Columbia University: Isis Rivero, Deputy Vice President for Facilities; Carlos Cortes, Project Manager, Facilities
__Architect__: Ellerbe Becket, New York:

Peter Pran, Design Principal and Senior Vice President; Jill Lerner, Project Manager, Senior Vice President; Eduardo Calma, Project Designer; Curtis Wagner, Project Designer; Tim Johnson, Project Designer; Carlos Zapata, Senior Designer and Vice President; Ray Skorupa, Project Manager; Tama Duffy, Interiors
__Laboratory Consultants__: GPR: Steve Rosenstein, Senior Partner
__Mechanical Engineers__: Cosentini: Marvin Mass, Senior Partner
__Photographer__: Maria Curran

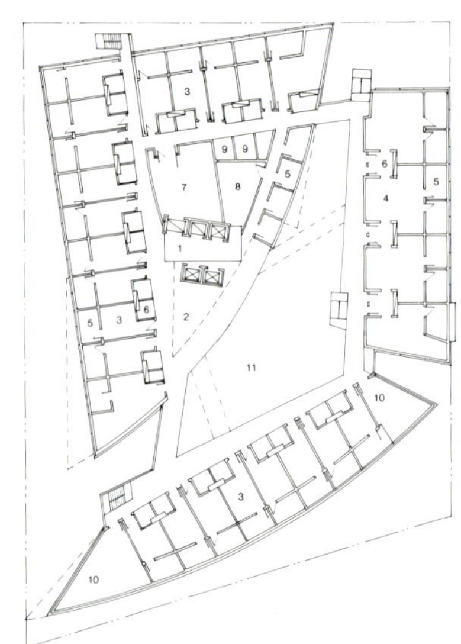

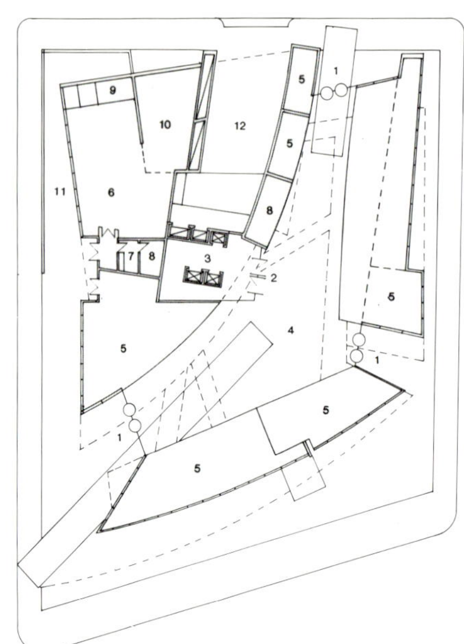

TYPICAL LABORATORY FLOOR PLAN
ENTRY LEVEL

BIN LADEN HEADQUARTERS
Jeddah, Saudi Arabia, 1990

The programme required a 16-storey headquarters, with 20,000 square feet per floor and a continuous atrium for the entire height of the building. The ground floor includes public and staff entries, as well as an executive entry, functioning exhibition space, mosque, auditorium and main general lobby. The executive floor, located on the 16th floor, includes a special executive office for the president, special prayer room and conference room adjacent to it, as well as executive offices for vice presidents. Floors two and three contain trading floors, while floors four to 15 contain general offices. The two building wings, one bent, one straight and pulled apart, allow for a dynamic central atrium and an expression of movement in the building articulation. The rectangular wing is clad in stone, and the bent, curved wing is clad in glass. Bridges and special conference rooms connect the two building wings, and activate the atrium.

Saudi Bin Laden Group: Sheikh Bakr Bin Laden, Chairman
Client Representative: Isaam Kronfol, Project Director
Architect: Ellerbe Becket, New York and Minneapolis: Peter Pran, Design Principal and Senior Vice President; Carlos Zapata, Vice President and Design Director; Mic Johnson, Vice President and Design Principal; Eduardo Calma, Project Designer; Paul Davis, Tim Johnston, Jeff Walden, Maria Wilthew, Berj Malikian, Lyn Rice, Designers; Robert Zumwalt, Vice President and Project Manager (First Phase); Deborah Stiefer, AES; Athene Carras, AES

Structural Engineer: Les Robertson, New York
Photographer: Dan Cornish

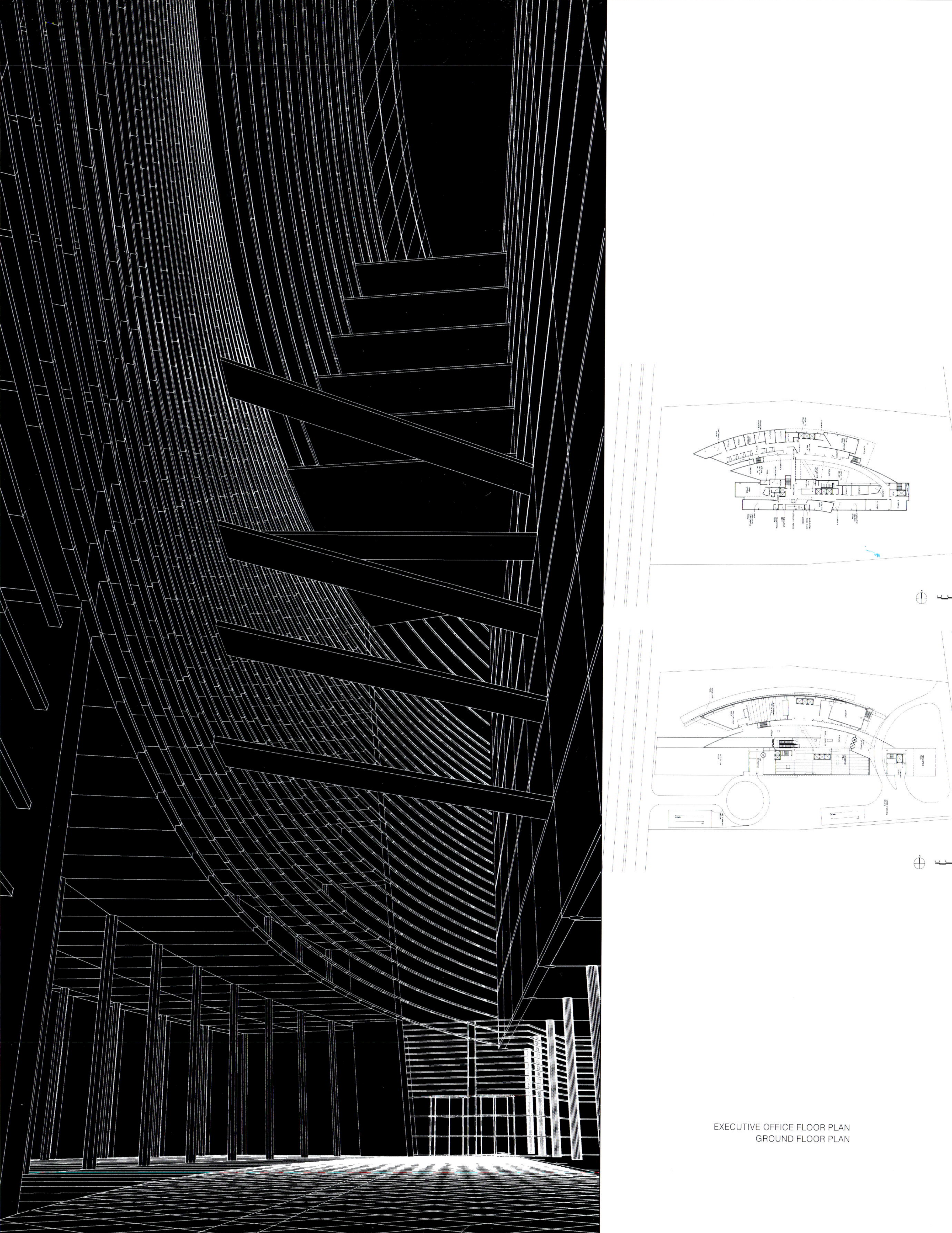

EXECUTIVE OFFICE FLOOR PLAN
GROUND FLOOR PLAN

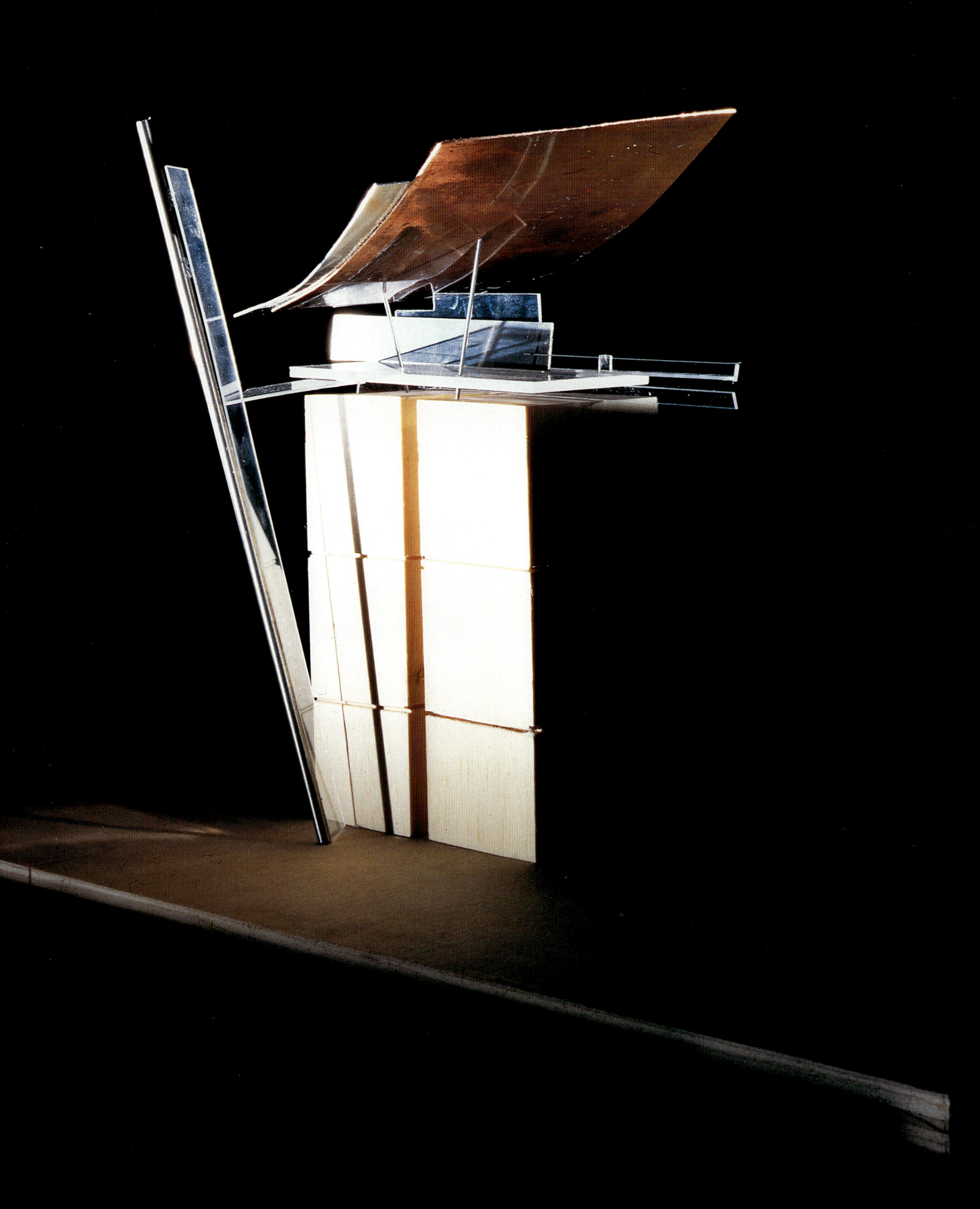

KING'S HILL DEVELOPMENT NEW TOWER ROOF AND TERRACE FOR MAIN ENTRY
West Malling, Kent, England, 1992

The King's Hill Development encompasses a beautiful, large area of the countryside in Kent, planned for office buildings, recreation centres, schools, shops, etc. The planners have a clear commitment to construct buildings that fully respect and enrich the site, landscape and surrounding existing buildings.

The older three-storey masonry towers are located adjacent to the main entry road to the entire King's Hill Development. On top of these two towers, an observation terrace with a protective roof above is planned. This terrace and its gentle, flowing roof shape give further articulation to the two existing towers and the main entry 'gate', as a spiritual and poetic symbol of the arrival to this progressive development. The new roof structure is fully respect- ful of the existing two towers, while expressing a feeling of movement and freedom.

__Client__: Rouse Kent Limited: Jay L Sholl, Director
__Architect__: Ellerbe Becket, New York: Peter Pran, Design Principal; Curtis Wagner, Project Designer
__Photographers__: Maria Curran, Mario Bettella

An installation inspired by the King's Hill Development scheme, created by Peter Pran for the 'Theory and Experimentation' Exhibition, Whiteley's, London, 1992

STATE UNIVERSITY OF NEW YORK
NEW ACADEMIC BUILDINGS
Binghamton, New York, USA, 1991-92

The commission is to design a 130,000 square foot new academic facility for the State University of New York at Binghamton in upstate New York. The building will serve as the new main entrance and 'Pedestrian Gateway' to the campus, receiving visitors and potential students as they approach the campus from the main parking areas. It houses SUNY Binghamton's School of Management, School of Nursing, School of Education and Human Development, Academic Computing Centre, research programmes, Undergraduate Admissions, shared Lecture Hall and Classrooms. Furthermore, it creates a new image for a university that is emerging as one of the leading liberal arts institutions nationally.

The selected two-building scheme, that is three storeys high, fits in with the existing three-storey buildings on campus (the main height throughout), and provides the desired exterior identity to the different departments. An interior connection between the new and the existing buildings further integrates the project and becomes part of SUNY Binghamton's 'winter campus' walkway. Building A contains mainly the School of Management and Undergraduate Admissions; and Building B contains mainly the School of Education and Human Development in its western wing and the School of Nursing in its eastern wing.

The entry to the Admissions Office, shared Lecture Halls and Classrooms is at Building A's curved tip, in its atrium which serves as the 'gateway' point. The existing campus is dominated by a series of rectangular buildings on a 90 degree grid. The two new buildings break the grid to create a dynamic and friendly expression of movement and freedom in its architectural statement. The large metal roof at the large Lecture Hall comes out of the ground, with its interior hall relating to both first and ground floors. The buildings will continue the concrete, tile and colour palette of the existing neighbouring science buildings and at the same time add copper, stainless steel and stone to give a material richness.

The goal stated by the client is to design a complex within tight budgetary constraints that fits in with the campus and at the same time brings in a new spirit and a new leading architecture of the highest quality.

Client: State University Construction Fund (SUCF) for the State University of New York at Binghamton (SUNY): (SUCF) Bob Ruckterstuhl, Manager of Design; Jim Biggane, Director of Consultant Design; Daryl Andreades, Associate Project Coordinator; (SUNY) Lois de Fleur, President; Michael Scullard, Vice President; Gene Gilliand, Assistant Vice President, Facilities; Larry Roma, Acting Assistant Vice President, Facilities; Gary Roodman, Acting Dean, SOM; Linda Biemer, Dean SEHD; Mary S Collins, Dean SON; Geof Gould, Admissions; Fred Brooks, Enrollment

Architects: Ellerbe Becket, New York: Peter Pran, Design Principal and Senior Vice President; Jill Lerner, Senior Vice President and Project Director; Lyn Rice, Project Architect/Designer; Carlos Zapata, Senior Designer and Vice President; Curtis Wagner, Project Designer; Eduardo Calma, Project Designer; Maria Wilthew, Designer; Timothy Johnson, Designer; Robert Zumwalt, Vice President and Project Manager; Robert Peralta, Project-Management; Brian McFarland, Computer Director; Diane Hayes, Interiors; Tama Duffy, Vice President and Interiors; Helen Ferguson, Designer; Gabriella Stamate, Technical; Joe Miou, Senior Technical Coordinator; Milton McCall, Technical; Louis Rivera, Technical; Kelly Vandeplasse, Technical; Ellerbe Becket, Washington, DC: Mike Jones, Educational Planning, Vice President and Design Principal

Mechanical/Electrical Engineers: Flack + Kurtz Engineers, New York: David Cooper; Tony Battaglia

Structural Engineer: Les Robertson, New York; Saw Teen See

Landscape Architect: Office of William Kuhl

Civil Engineer: Ysrael Seinuk, PC

Photographers: Dan Cornish, Maria Curran

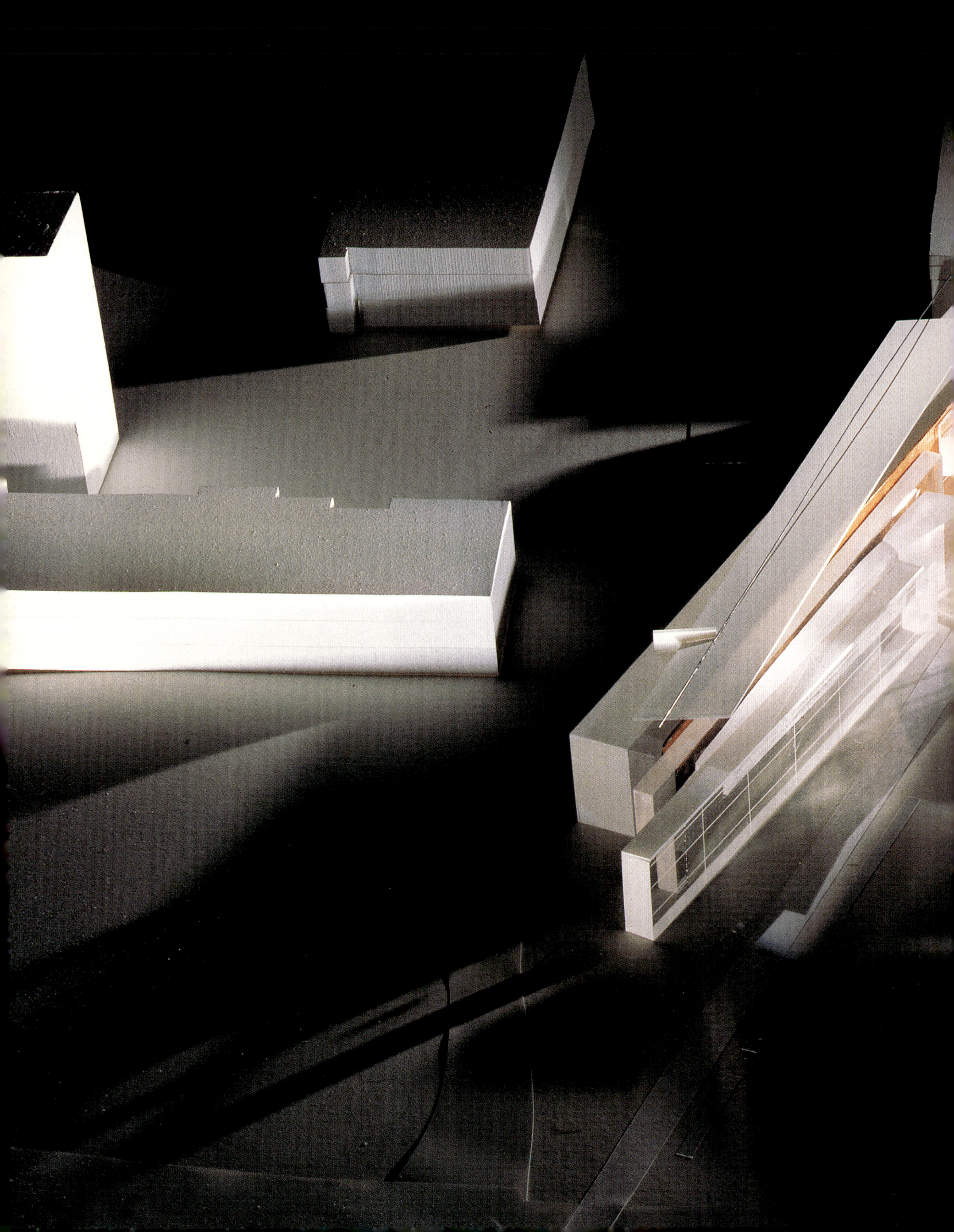

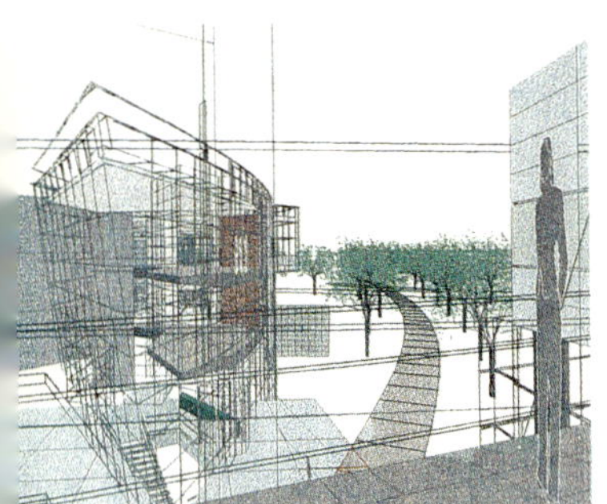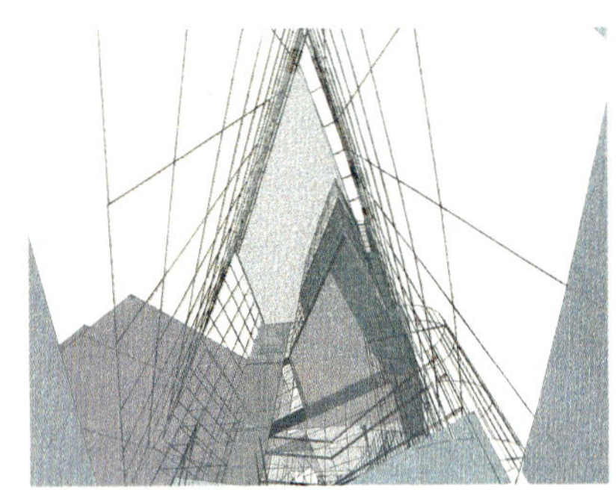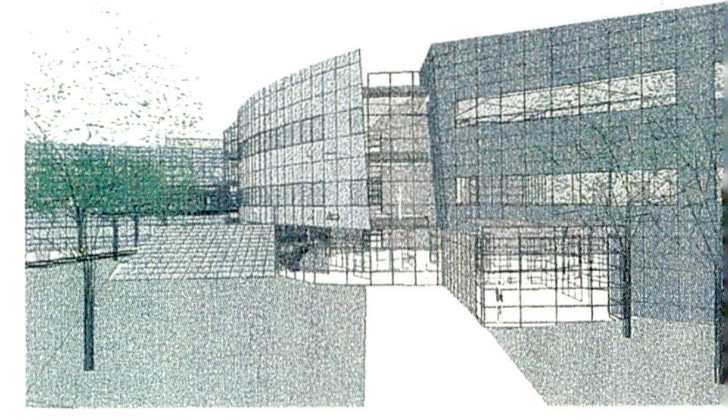

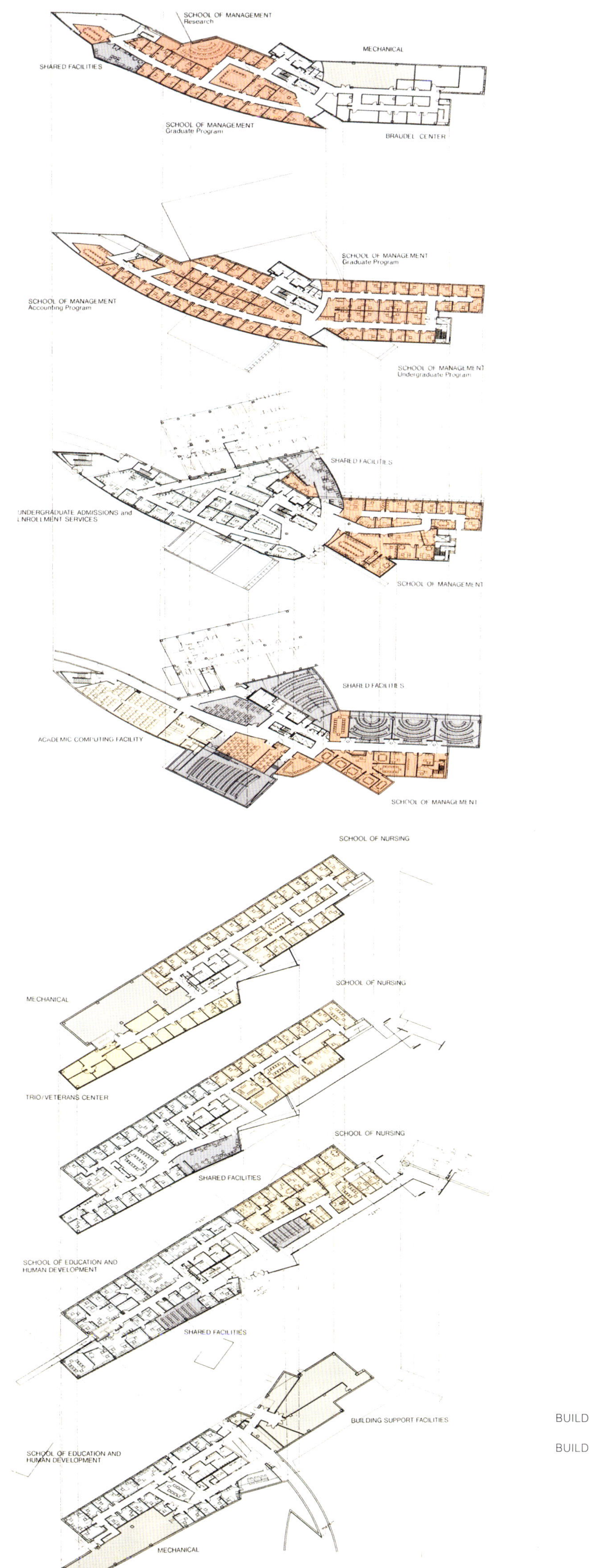

BUILDING A: THIRD, SECOND, FIRST
AND GROUND FLOOR PLANS
BUILDING B: THIRD, SECOND, FIRST
AND GROUND FLOOR PLANS

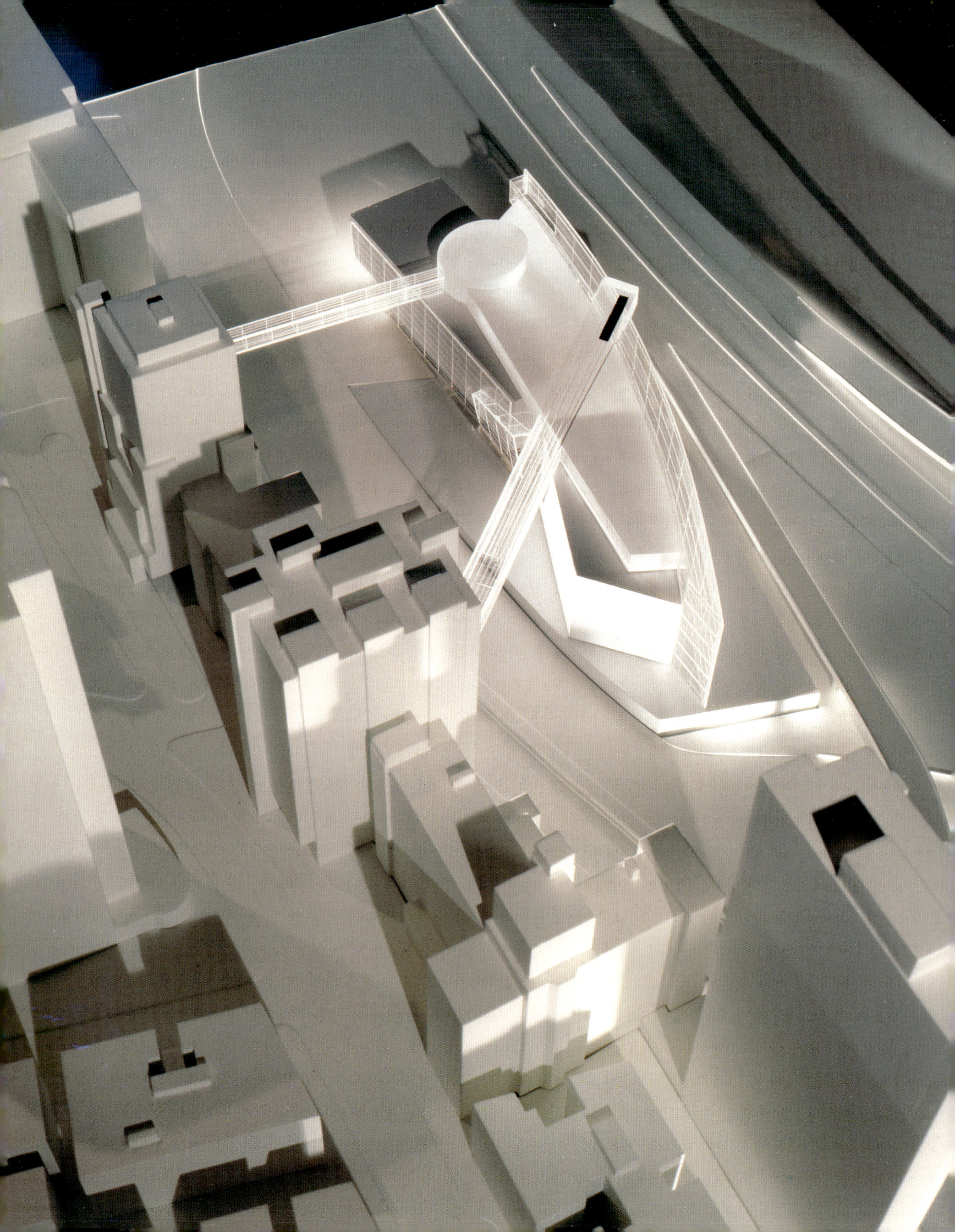

NEW YORK PSYCHIATRIC INSTITUTE

Manhattan, New York, USA, 1992

The new Psychiatric Institute is located on an urban site, west of Riverside Drive in Manhattan; it will be connected to adjacent buildings in the Columbia Presbyterian Medical/Research Complex via bridges across Riverside Drive. Laboratories will be connected to the Kolb Annex research tower at the north end of the site; inpatient areas will be connected to the Milstein Pavilion of Presbyterian Hospital at the south end. Due to the prominent location of the site as one enters the city from the George Washington Bridge, a high-quality design addressing key urban design and community issues is paramount.

The site is exceptional with magnificent views of the Hudson River, the George Washington Bridge and the northern end of Manhattan. The overall building configuration maintains a low profile at a total height of six storeys above Riverside Drive. This will allow an open view corridor to the Hudson River from the neighbourhood around 168th Street pending future removal of the old NYPI building. The new building will allow public access in two locations: primary entry via automobile arrival will be located off Riverside Drive; pedestrians from the neighbourhood and from city transit locations at a higher elevation will enter via lobby space existing in the Institute's Kolb Research Facility, with access through a pedestrian bridge link to the new facility. The entry on Riverside Drive will also be formed by an open plaza, which will graciously lead into the existing natural landscape to the south of the building. The overall building shape is defined by a laboratory research wing to the north, and an inpatient and outpatient wing to the south. A six-storey atrium unifies the two wings and becomes the focal point of both grade and bridge circulation. In addition, the western facade takes the form of a gentle, curving wall which unites the two programmatic masses, gracefully defining its presence within the site.

The New York Psychiatric Institute is the oldest psychiatric research facility in the country and is one of the pre-eminent psychiatric institutes in the USA and the world. It is funded by New York State and receives \$35 million annually in federal and private grants for studies in areas such as schizophrenia, substance abuse, behavioural aspects of HIV, anxiety disorders, eating disorders and numerous other programmes. Design requirements demand state-of-the-art technology and flexibility in the design of laboratory and research spaces due to the constantly changing nature of research grants.

In addition to laboratory research space, the new facility will house 72 inpatient psychiatric research beds, as well as a significant education and training component, a 24-bed community service inpatient unit, a public school for children being treated at the Institute, a state-of-the-art animal holding facility for transgenic mice, and administrative and support spaces. The project also includes a new power plant for the complex, and a 100 car parking garage below the new building.

Client: New York State Office of Mental Health (OMH): Mr CC Hommel; Mr David Beemer
Facilities Development Corporation (FDC): Ms Norma Roca, Development Administrator
New York Psychiatric Institute: Dr John Oldham, Director; Mr Steven Papp, Deputy Administrator; Mr Hal Seligson, Director of Business Office
Architects: Ellerbe Becket, New York: Jill Lerner, Project Director; Peter Pran, Design Principal; Timothy Johnson, Project Designer; Curtis Wagner, Designer; Lyn Rice, Designer; Bill Kidd, Senior Medical Planner; Don Velsey, Senior Medical Planner; Xenia Urban, Senior Medical Planner; Laura Ettelman, Project Architect; Ellerbe Becket, Washington DC: Rich Lincicome, Administrative Principal; Mark Molen, Project Designer; Mike Jones, Consultant Design Principal
Engineers: Seelye Stevenson, Value & Knecht, New York: George Nagelberg, Chief Engineer and Principal
Laboratory Consultants: GPR, New York: Steve Rosenstein, Partner
Environmental Consultant: Ethan C Eldon Associates: Ethan Eldon Principal
Photographer: Dan Cornish

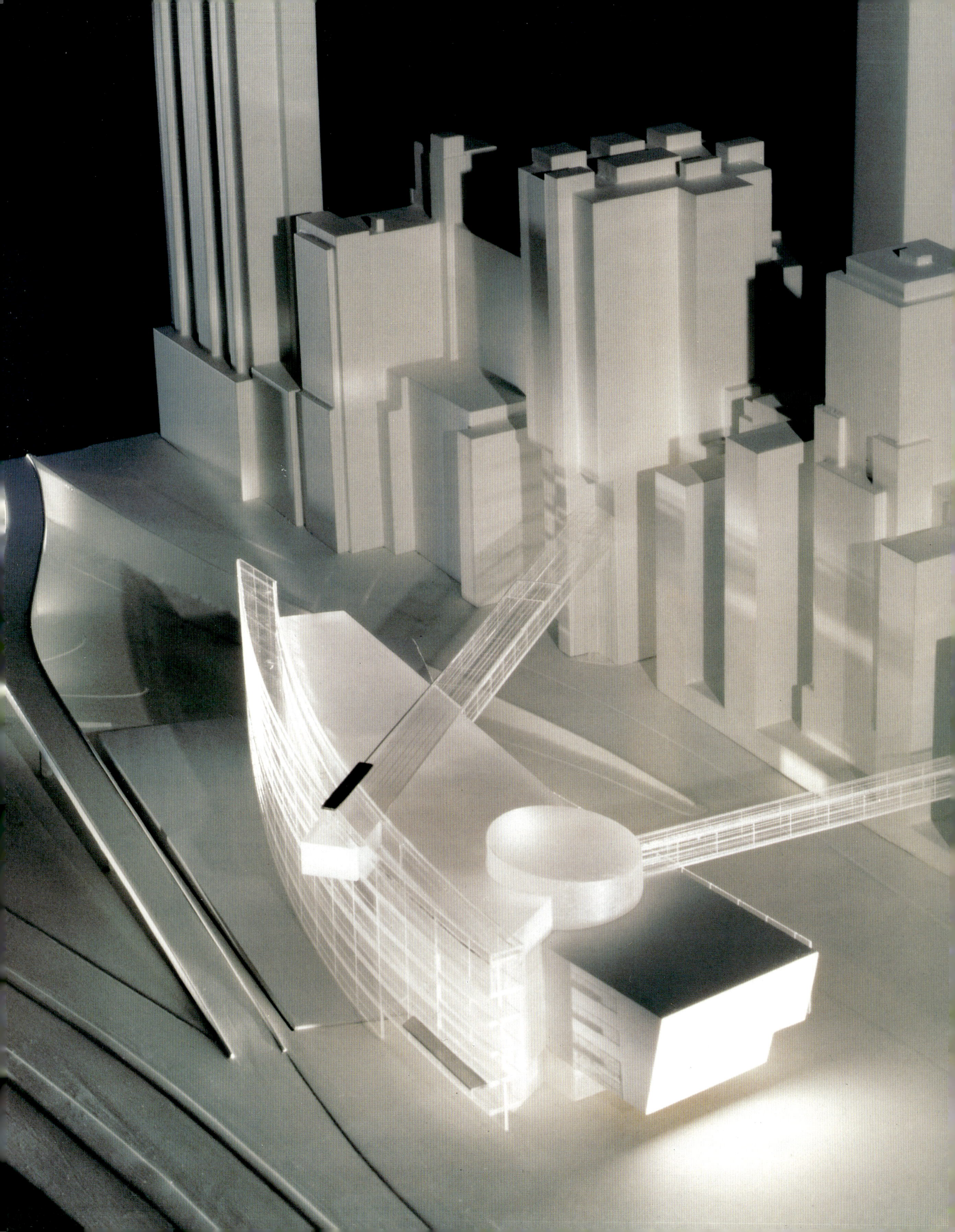

SITE PLAN

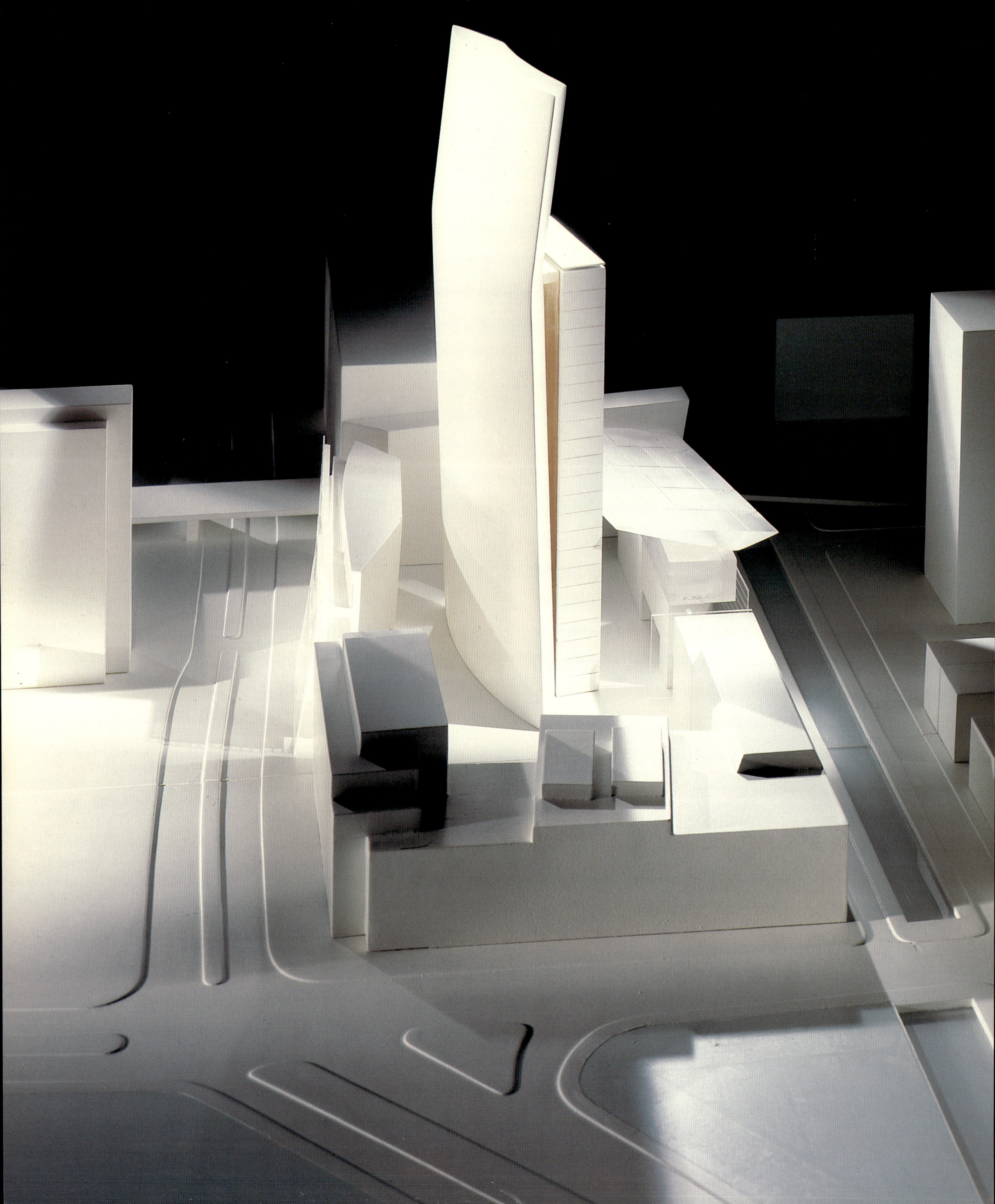

DE CENTRALE LOKATIE IN DEN HAAG

The Hague, The Netherlands, 1992

Situated on a major site downtown, next to the main railway station and the city's largest park, this 35-storey office highrise, with an eight-storey lowrise and multi-functional atrium space, will be the tallest building in The Hague.

The client's aim was to provide a modern highrise complex of the highest architectural quality that would contextually respect the city and at the same time represent an innovative and new modern statement. The complex shows respect for and reference to both the older Parliament buildings and Richard Meier's new City Hall.

These four design schemes were presented to the client, each representing a highly refined and poetic solution in this city; a site-specific solution.

***Client**: Maatschappij voor Bedrijfsobjecten nv (MBO) Amsterdam, The Netherlands: Jan Doets, President; Jaap Joldersma, Project Director; JAM Hensbergen; E Stomp and the City of Hague; Peter Noordanus, Mayor/ Alderman; Peter Verschuren; Ad Alderliesten*
***Architects**: Ellerbe Becket, CCI New York and CCI Minneapolis; Peter Pran, Design Principal and Senior Vice President; Carlos Zapata, Design Principal, Design Studio, New York; Eduardo Calma, Project Designer; Curtis Wagner, Project Designer; Tim Johnson, Project Designer; Jeff Walden, Project Designer; Paul Davis, Project Designer; David Koenen, Designer; Dorman Anderson, Principal NBBJ, co-presenter with Pran at first interview, of Ellerbe Becket, NBBJ credentials*
***Architect Collaborator**: Jo Coenen, Maastricht, The Netherlands*
***Modelmaker**: Richard Tenguerian*
***Photographer**: Dan Cornish*

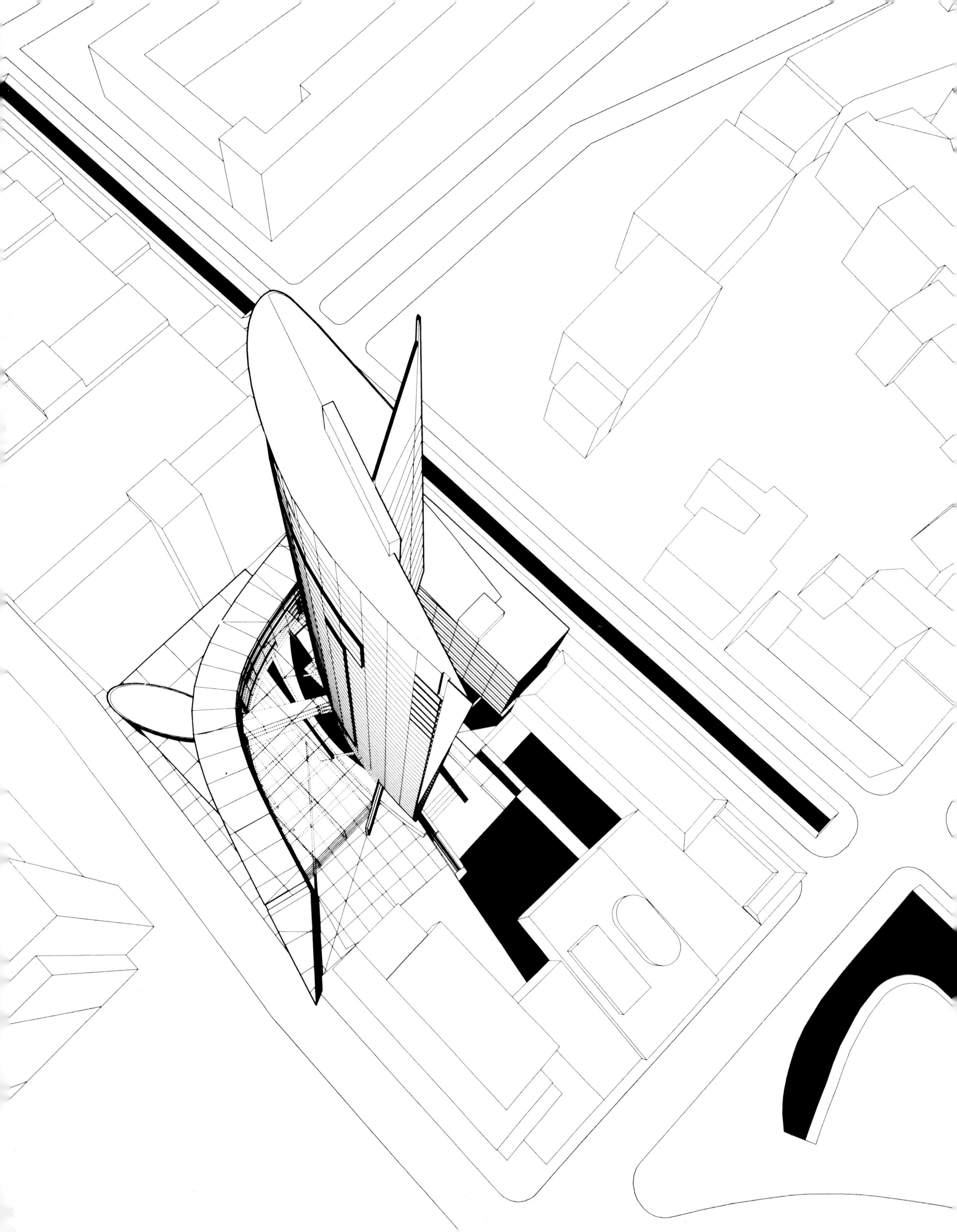

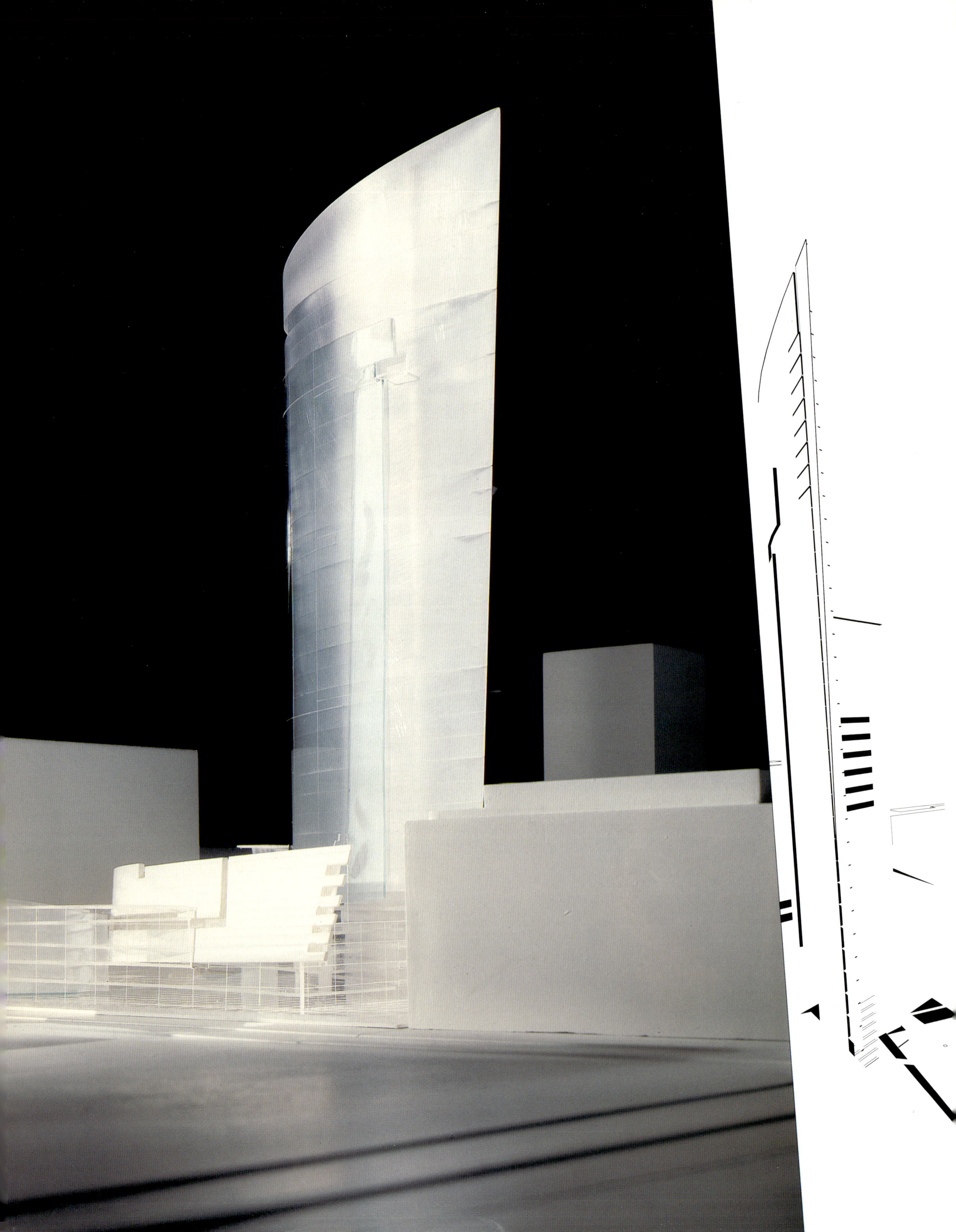

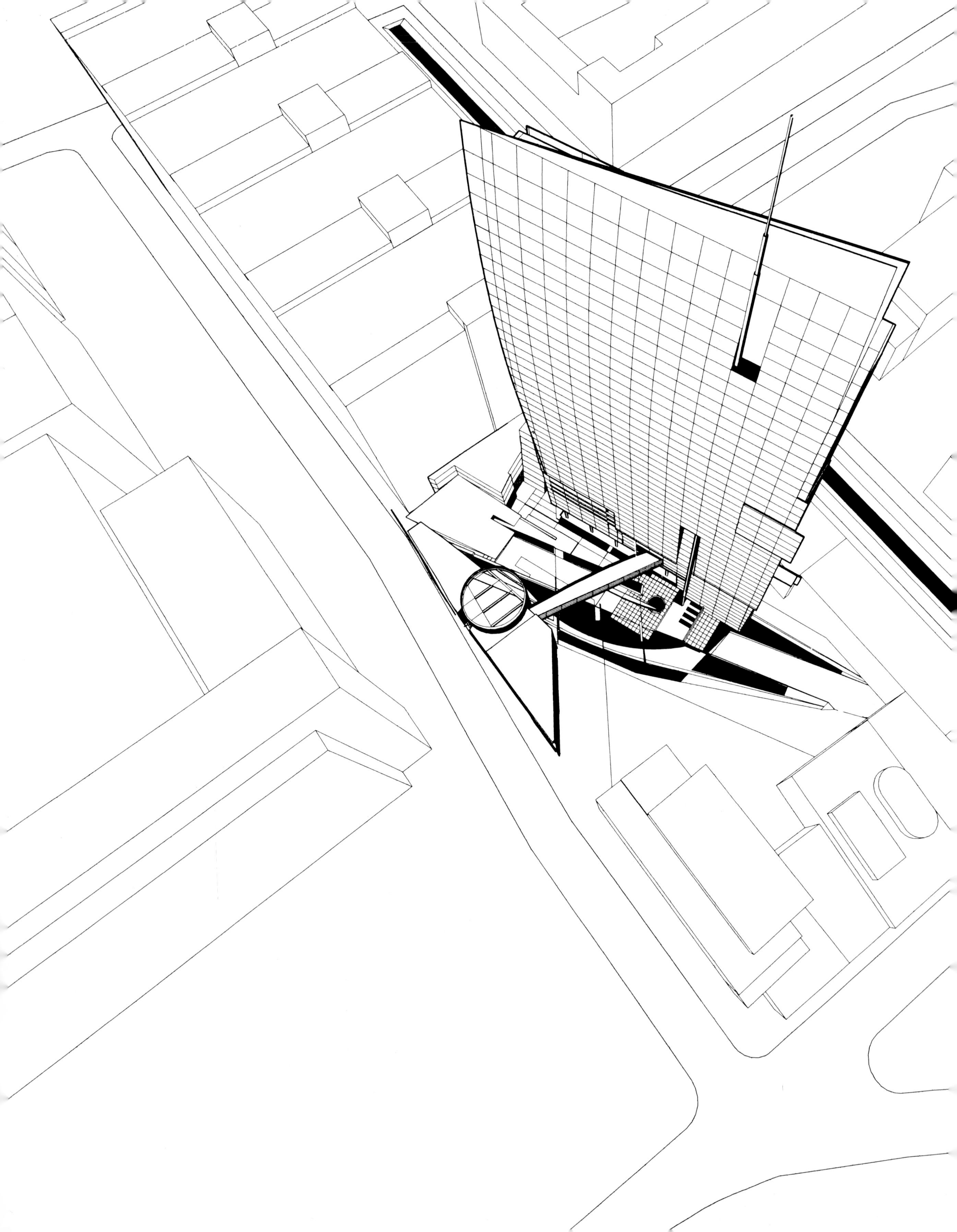

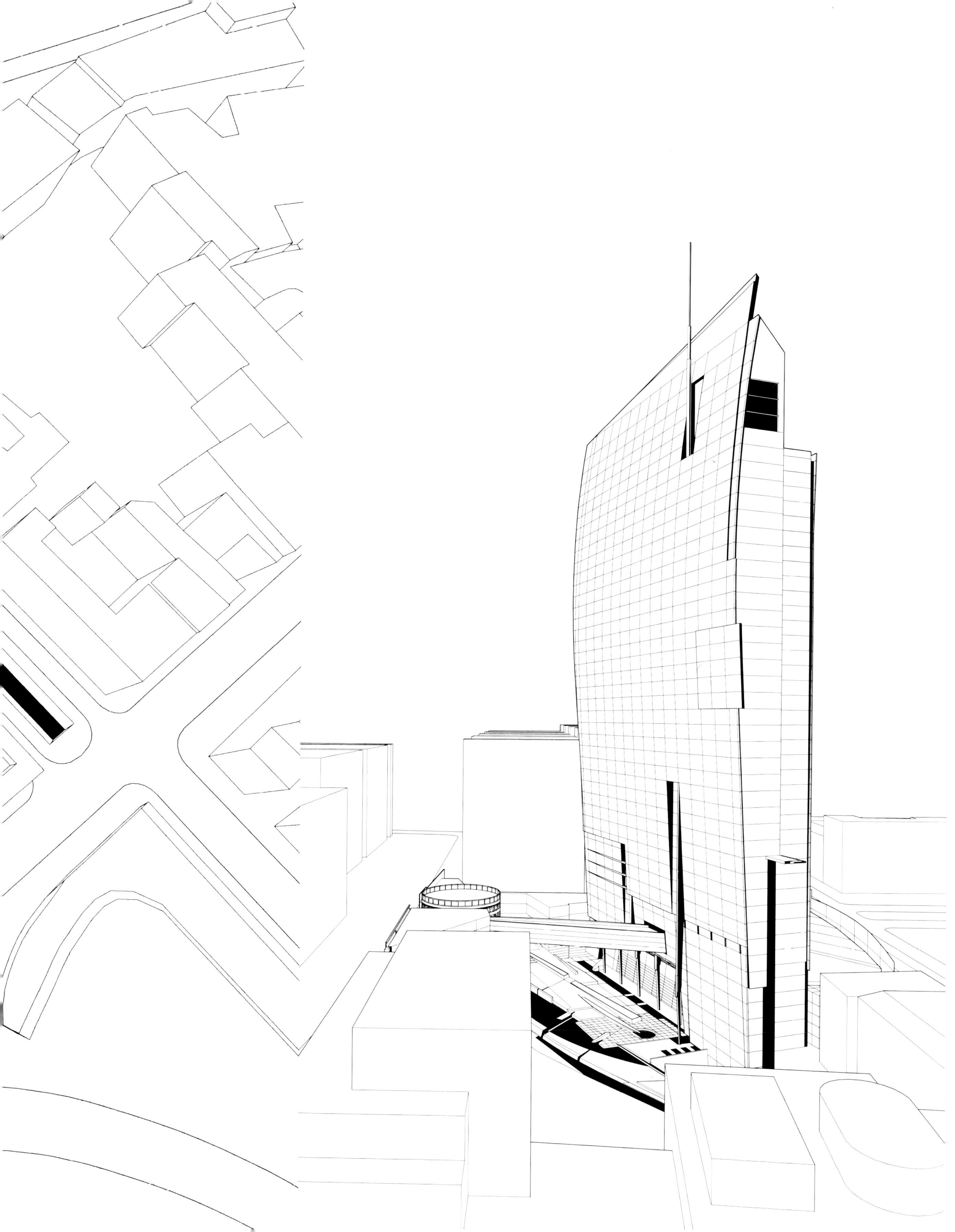

CORPORATE HEADQUARTERS BUILDING
Jeddah, Saudi Arabia, 1992

This new 90,000 m square headquarters for a major Saudi Arabian corporation is located on a magnificent site on the Red Sea, along the Corniche Boulevard, in Jeddah. The highrise complex accommodates 2,500 employees with office space, 2,000 car parking garage, and special amenities including a mosque. The complex meets all the functional requirements and provides an excellent environment for staff and visitors. At the same time, the new building design concept gives a new and dignified image, representative of the company and the Kingdom of Saudi Arabia's tremendous progress on the eve of the 21st century.

The highrise complex consists of two vertical wings that enclose a beautiful, full height atrium. The building wing facing the Red Sea and the Corniche, takes the sail-like form of a gentle curve. The inside face of the curve gives the atrium a graceful, exuberant quality. The rectangular inland wing serves as a foil for this dramatic curve. The goal is to provide a building design that will be completely respectful of and appropriate for the city of Jeddah, and at the same time achieve an architectural design of the highest quality internationally.

The client explicitly desires a landmark building, and thinks this design fully meets that goal. This headquarters might be recognised as one of the most innovative and original highrise designs of the next decade.

Client: Saudi Bin Laden Group, Jeddah, Saudi Arabia: Sheikh Bakr Bin Laden, Chairman; Sheikh Saleh Bin Laden; Samir F Ataya
Architect: Ellerbe Becket, Minneapolis and New York: William D Chilton, Project Director; Peter Pran, Design Principal; Ted Davis, Senior Project Designer; Pat Bougie, Project Architect; Tim Johnson, Designer; Jeff Walden, Designer; Scott Saunders, Structural Engineer; Brian Benson, Mechanical Engineer; Tom Crew, Electrical Engineer; David Loehr, Planner; Doug Renier, Civil Engineer
Photographer: Dan Cornish

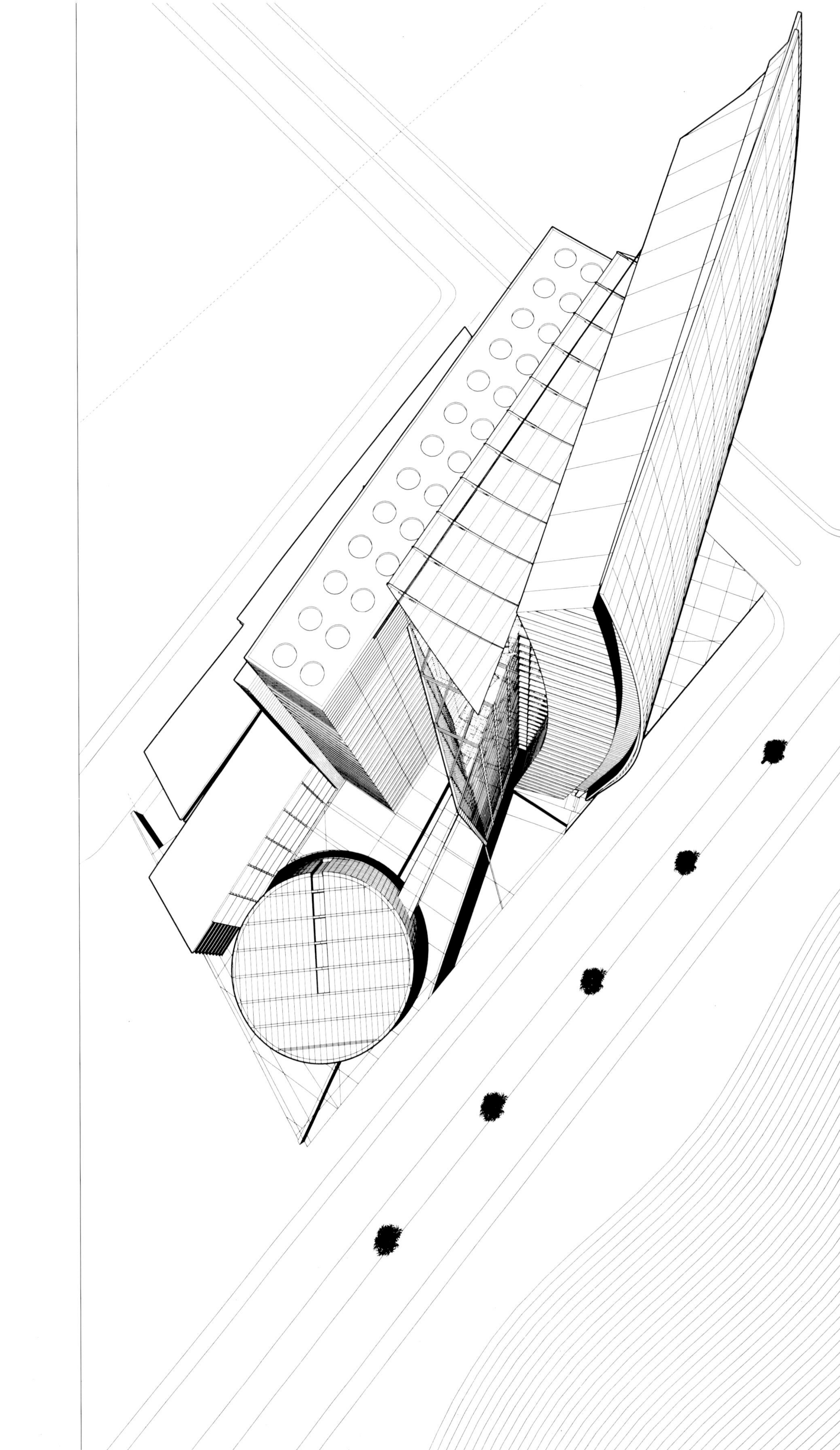

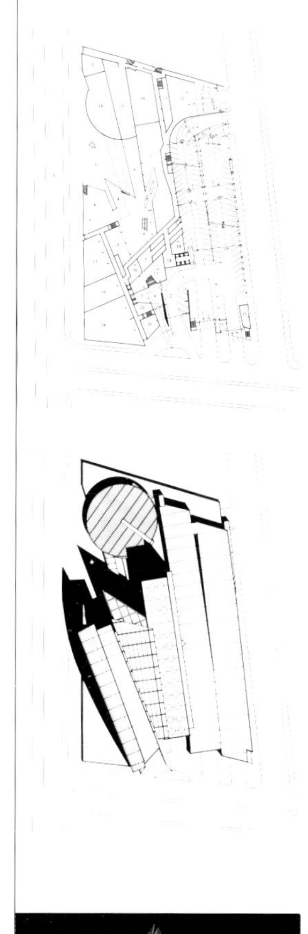

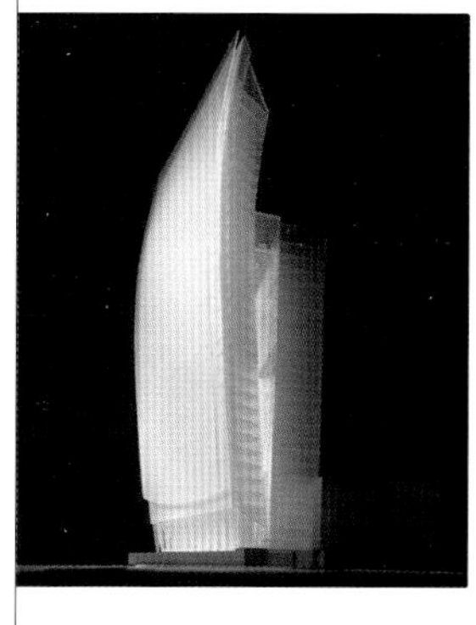

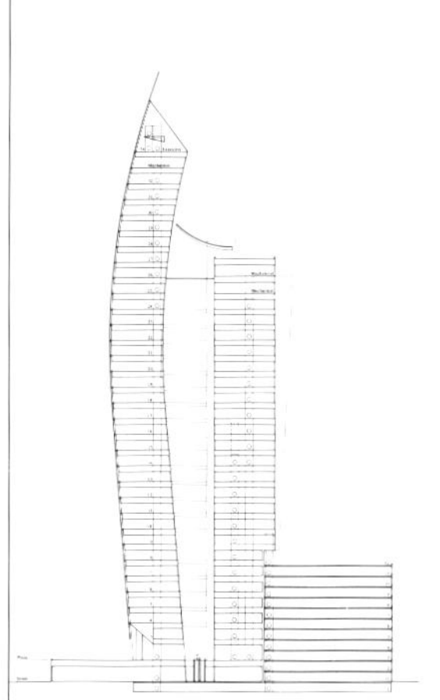

STREET LEVEL PLAN
SITE PLAN

SECTION

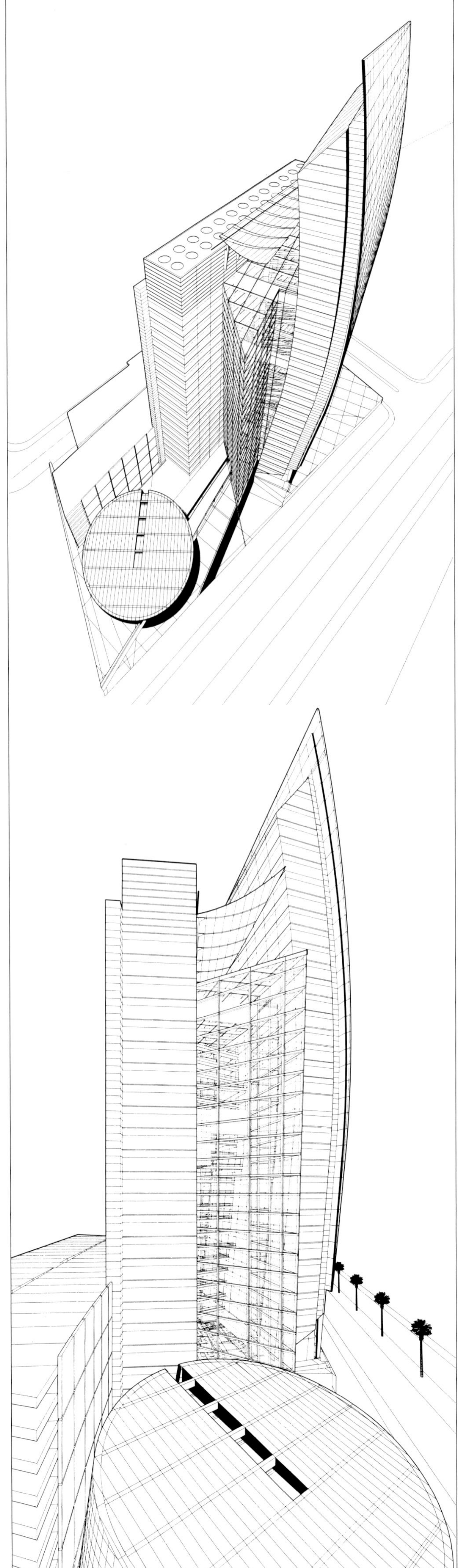

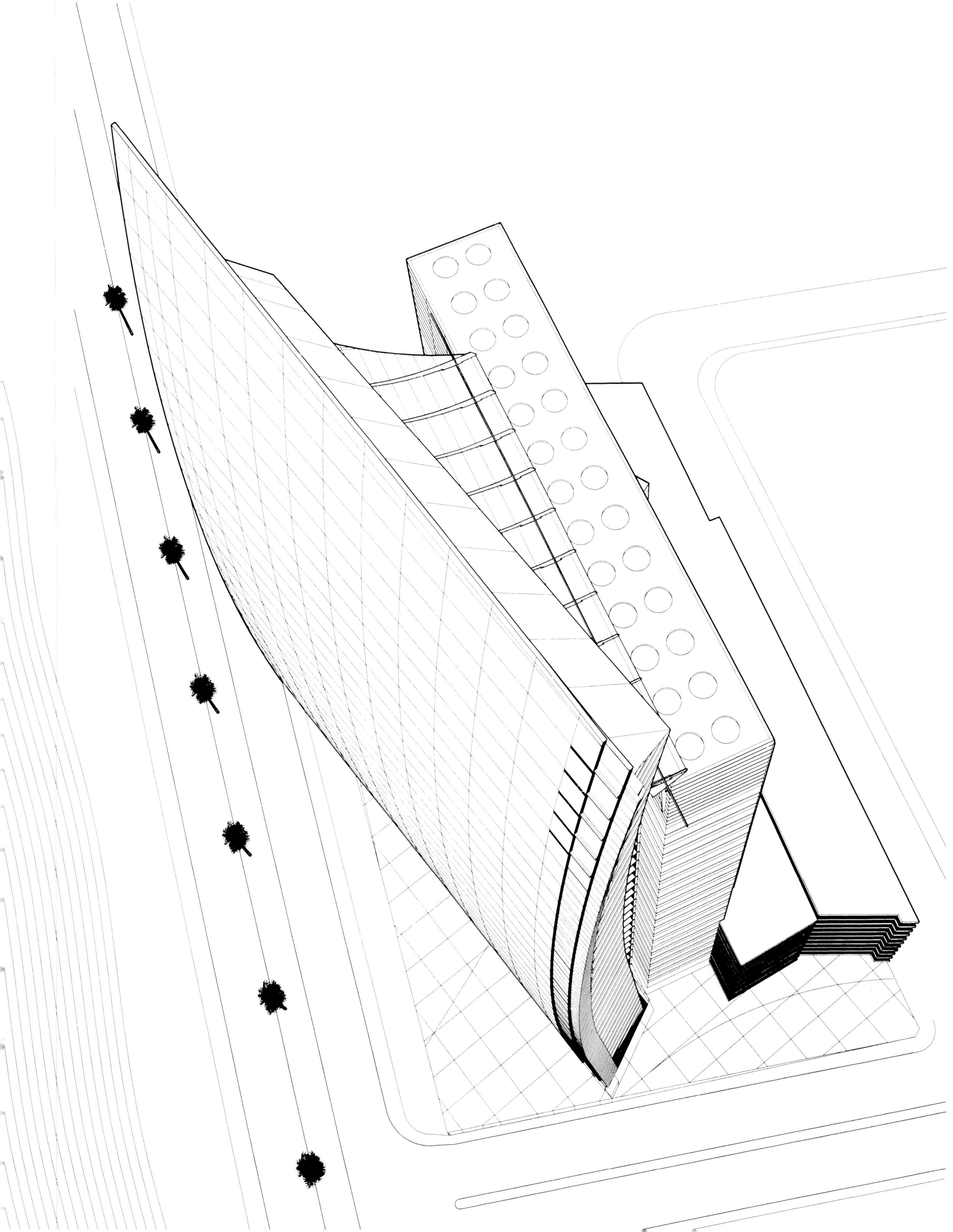

Chair, 1962, designed by Peter Pran

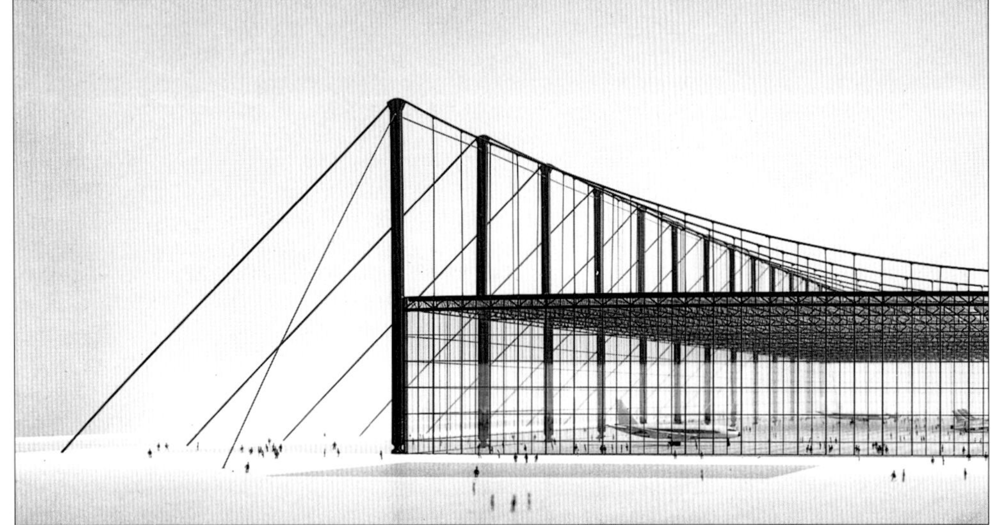

Exhibition Hall, Chicago, Illinois, 1969 by Peter Pran, developed as part of his Master of Science in Architecture degree from Illinois Institute of Technology (advisors: Myron Goldsmith, Fazlur Khan and David Sharpe)

Facilities Center, Methodist Hospital of Indiana, Indianapolis, Indiana (Architects SGE: Peter Pran, Design Director; Warren Hendrichson, Designer)

BIOGRAPHY

Peter Pran

Born in Oslo, Norway
1961 Bachelor of Architecture, Arkitekthögskole University, Oslo
1969 Master of Science in Architecture, Illinois Institute of Technology, Chicago, Illinois, USA

Professional Positions

1961 Architect/Designer, Tore Moxness, Stockholm
1961-63 Architect/Project Designer, Nils Holter, Oslo
1963-66 Architect and Project Designer, Mies van der Rohe, FAIA, Chicago
1966-69 Architect and Project Designer, Skidmore, Owings & Merrill, Chicago
1969-73 Partner, Anderson & Pran, Pullman, Washington
1973-77 Senior Architect/Senior Designer, Skidmore, Owings & Merrill, Chicago
1977-82 Director of Design and Associate, Schmidt, Garden & Erikson, Chicago
1982-84 Director of Design and Associate Partner, The Grad Partnership, Newark, New Jersey
1984-85 Project Design Director and Associate Principal, Russo + Sonder, New York
1985-86 Project Design Director and Associate Principal, Eli Attia Architects, New York
1986-Present Design Principal and Senior Vice President, Ellerbe Becket, New York

Academic Positions

1969-73 Assistant Professor, Washington State University, Pullman, Washington
1973-81 Adjunct Associate Professor, University of Illinois, Chicago
1981-82 Visiting Associate Professor, University of Illinois, Urbana-Champaign, Illinois
1983-86 Adjunct Associate Professor, New Jersey Institute of Technology, Newark, New Jersey
1984 Visiting Professor, University of Palermo, Palermo (with NYIT)
1985-1990 Distinguished Adjunct Professor of Architecture, New York Institute of Technology, Old Westbury, New York

1990 Visiting Professor of Architecture, Kanto Gakuin University, Yokohama, Japan
1993 Visiting Faculty, Royal Danish Academy of Fine Arts, School of Architecture, Copenhagen, Denmark

Selected Buildings and Projects

1962 New National TV Building, Oslo
1963 National Gallery, Berlin (with Mies van der Rohe)
1965 Chicago Federal Center, Chicago (with Mies van der Rohe)
1966 Toronto Dominion Center, Toronto (with Mies van der Rohe)
1968 CTA Rapid Transit Stations, Chicago
1972 KRPL Radio & Television Station and Offices, Moscow, Idaho
1973 Khaneh Center, Tehran
1976 Jeddah International Airport, Jeddah, Saudi Arabia
1976 Diamond-Shamrock Headquarters, Concord Township, Ohio
1979 Emergency Wing, Methodist Hospital, Gary, Indiana
1979 Recreation Center, Marian College, Fond du Lac, Wisconsin
1980 Family Health Center, Gary, Indiana
1982 Facilities Center, Indianapolis, Indiana
1983 Codex Headquarters, Mansfield, Massachusetts
1984 Prudential Short Hills Office Complex, Short Hills, New Jersey
1986 233 Park Avenue South, New York
1987 South Ferry Plaza, New York
1987 New Hartford City Hall, Hartford, Connecticut
1988 Headquarters for Schibsted Gruppen newspapers Aftenposten and Verdens Gang, Oslo
1988 New Consolidated Terminal for American Airlines/Northwest Airlines, JFK International Airport, New York
1990 Deloitte & Touche Headquarters, Wilton, Connecticut
1990 Canadian National/Royal Trust Development, Toronto
1990 CN/Labatts Headquarters, TV Studios, Toronto
1990 New Chicago Stadium and McCormick Place Addition,

Chicago
1991 Boston Gardens Arena, Boston, Massachusetts
1991 Banco Popular, Quito and Ibarra, Ecuador
1991 Resort Hotel, Okinawa, Japan
1991 New Rikshospital, Oslo
1991 Columbia University, Research Center for Disease Prevention, New York
1992 New Academic Buildings, State University of New York at Binghamton, New York
1992 Staten Island Development Center, Staten Island, New York
1990-92 Corporate Headquarters, Jeddah, Saudi Arabia
1992 New Entry, Kings Hill Development, Kent, England
1992 New York Psychiatric Institute, New York
1992 De Centrale in Den Haag, The Hague, The Netherlands
1992 New York Police Academy, The Bronx, New York

Awards and Honours

1976 Illinois State AIA Service Award, for co-authoring book 100 Years of Architecture in Chicago: Continuity of Structure and Form, *and co-organising exhibit on same subject*
1977 Outstanding New Citizen Award, from Citizenship Council of Metropolitan Chicago
1977 Distinguished Building Design Award, Chicago Chapter AIA, and Building Design Honor Award, Illinois Council AIA, for Museum in Chicago
1978 First Prize in Chicago Townhouse Competition, sponsored by Graham Foundation
1980 National Design Awards, from Architectural Record, UCLA, Columbia University and AIA Health Care Program for Family Health Center, Gary, Indiana and for Petersburg Psychiatric Institute, Petersburg, Virginia
1981 Award Mention for Facilities Center, Indianapolis, from Chicago Architectural Club
1981 Second Prize in Architectural Competition for Pittsburgh Center for the Arts Addition, Pittsburgh, Pennsylvania

1982 Design Award for Recreation Building, Marian College, Wisconsin, from Chicago Architectural Club
1983 Second Prize in National Design Competition, Codex Corporation Headquarters, Mansfield, Massachusetts
1984 National Design Award, Passaic County Juvenile Detention Facility, Haledon, New Jersey, from National AIA and ACA
1986 Design Honor Award from New York Chapter/American Institute of Architects, for Entry and Lobby, 233 Park Avenue South, New York
1987 Design Honor Award, New York Chapter, American Institute of Architects, for South Ferry Plaza, New York
1988 Design Award, New York Chapter/American Institute of Architects, for New Hartford City Hall, Hartford, Connecticut
1988 Honorary Citizen of Minnesota (appointed by Governor Perpich)
1988-89 First Prize, International/ National Architecture Competition 1988 and Progressive Architecture Design Award 1989, and New York Chapter/American Institute of Architects Design Award, 1989 for Schibsted-Ditten Project, Headquarters for Aftenposten and Verdens Gang newspapers, Oslo, 1989
1989 The NYC/AIA Design Jury 1989 gave three 'Special Awards for Body of Work' to Richard Meier (for three projects); to Peter Eisenmann (for three projects) and to Ellerbe Becket – with Peter Pran, Design Principal, (for three projects)
1989-90 National Design Award from American Collegiate Schools of Architecture, 1990 and New York Chapter, American Institute of Architects Design Award, 1989, for Consolidated Terminal for American Airlines/Northwest Airlines, John F Kennedy International Airport, New York
1991 First Prize, International/ National Architecture Competition, 1989, and New York Chapter, American Institute of Architects

Design Award, 1990 and Progressive Architecture *Design Award 1991*, for CN/Royal Trust Office Complex, Toronto
1991 Design Award, New York Chapter, American Institute of Architects, for Banco Popular, Quito, Ecuador
1991 Design Award, New York Chapter, American Institute of Architects, for New Rikshospital, Oslo
1992 National AIA Interior Design Award of Excellence, 1992, and Interior Design Award, New York Chapter, American Institute of Architects, 1990, for Deloitte & Touche Headquarters, Wilton, Connecticut

Exhibits

1973 100 Years of Architecture in Chicago, *Neue Sammlung Museum, Munich*
1975 150 Year Anniversary of Norwegian Immigrants, *One Illinois Center, Chicago*
1976 100 Years of Architecture in Chicago: Continuity of Structure and Form, *Museum of Contemporary Art, Chicago*
1978 Town Houses by 19 Chicago Architects, *Graham Foundation, Chicago and Walker Art Center, Minneapolis*
1979 Urban Open Spaces, *Cooper-Hewitt Museum, New York*
1980 Chicago Tribune Tower – Late Entries, *Museum of Contemporary Art, Chicago; La Jolla Museum of Contemporary Art, Los Angeles; Fort Worth Art Center, Fort Worth; San Francisco Museum of Modern Art, San Francisco; Chicago Historical Society, Chicago (1982)*
1980 Creation and Recreation: American Dreams, *Jugend Hall Museum, Helsinki*
1981 Chicago Architectural Drawings, *Frumkin-Struve Gallery, Chicago, and at the University of Tennessee (1982)*
1981 Chicago Architectural Club – First Annual Exhibition, *Graham Foundation, Chicago*
1981 Architectural Drawings by Peter Pran and Kenneth Schroder, *Frumkin-Struve Gallery, Chicago*

1981 New Chicago Architecture, *Palazzo Gran Guardia Vecchia/ Museo di Castelvecchio, Verona, Italy; Art Museum, Palermo, Italy; Art Institute of Chicago, Chicago (1983)*
1982 Architectural Drawings by Peter Pran, *Allan Frumkin Gallery, New York*
1982 Chicago Architects Design, *The Art Institute of Chicago, Chicago*
1983 Variations on a Theme: Carnegie Mansion, *Cooper-Hewitt Museum, New York*
1984 Revisionist Modernism and Post-Modern Architecture 1960-80; *Deutsches Architekturmuseum, Frankfurt; Pompidou Centre, Paris, (1985); IMB Art Gallery, New York (1987)*
1984 150 Years of Chicago Architecture, *Ecole des Beaux-Arts and Paris Art Centre, Paris; Museum of Science and Industry, Chicago (1985)*
1986 New Directions in American Architecture, *exhibited in 160 US embassies internationally, sponsored by United States Information Agency, Washington DC*
1986 Modernism Redux: Critical Alternatives for Architecture in the Next Decade, *Grey Art Gallery, New York University, New York*
1986 International Exhibit of Architectural Drawings, *Max Protetch Gallery, New York*
1987 NYC/AIA Designs Awards Exhibit, *National Academy of Design (Smithsonian Institute), New York*
1988 NYC/AIA Designs Awards Exhibit, *National Academy of Design, New York*
1988 New York Architects, *Palazzo Chiaramonte, Enna, Italy; Skala Gallery, Copenhagen; University of Los Andes, Bogota, Columbia (1989); University of Merida, Merida, Venezuela (1989); Museum of Finnish Architecture, Helsinki (1989); Gallery of Art, Quito, Ecuador (1989); International Design Center, Queens, New York (1989); Pratt Institute, Brooklyn, New York (1989)*
1989 The Architecture of Peter Pran & Carlos Zapata of Ellerbe

Becket, *ROM Gallery, Oslo*
1989 New York Architecture 1970-1990, *Deutsches Architekturmuseum, Frankfurt; Contemporary Museum, Madrid, 1990; Taipai Fine Arts Museum, Taiwan, 1991*
1990 NYC/AIA Design Awards Exhibit, *Whitney Museum Downtown Gallery, New York*
1990 Communicating Ideas Artfully, *opening exhibit at NEOCON, Merchandise Mart, Chicago, curated by Thomas Fisher, Executive Editor, Progressive Architecture*
1991 NYC/AIA Design Awards Exhibit, *New York Historical Society, New York*
1991 Contemporary Architectural Drawings, *100 Years Anniversary Exhibit, Avery Hall, Columbia University, New York*
1992 Theory & Experimentation, *Royal Institute of British Architects Gallery and Whiteleys, London, sponsored by the Academy Group, RIBA and The Royal Academy of Arts*

Visiting Jury Member and Critic at Universities

Columbia University, New York, 1984-1990
Harvard University, Boston, 1986 and 1992
Tulane University, New Orleans 1989
Pratt Institute, New York, International Seminar, Summer 1990
Parsons School of Design, 1990
Observation Member, National Accrediting Team reviewing Columbia University School of Architecture, 1988
One of three finalists for Dean of Architecture position, Pratt Institute, Spring 1991

Jury Member

On Jury for international architecture competition for New Art & Media Cultural Center (ZKM), Karlsruhe, Germany, 1989
San Diego, California, AIA Annual Design Awards Jury, 1989
Iowa AIA State Chapter Annual Design Awards Jury, 1989
Portland AIA Chapter Annual

Design Awards Jury, 1989
Seattle AIA Chapter AIA Annual Design Awards Jury, 1990
Virginia AIA State Chapter Annual Design Awards Jury, 1991
Washington DC AIA Chapter Annual Design Awards Jury, 1991
Los Angeles AIA Chapter Annual Design Awards Jury, 1991
NIAE, Paris Prize Jury (in New York), 1992

Lectures

Technical University, Helsinki,1980
University of Wisconsin, Milwaukee, Wisconsin,1981
Ball State University, Indiana,1982
University of Palermo, Sicily,1984
NTH University, Trondheim,1988
Walker Art Center, Minneapolis, Minnesota, 1988
Oslo Arkitekthögskole, Oslo,1989
Catholic University, Washington DC,1989
Iowa AIA State Convention, Des Moines, Iowa,1989
Tulane University, New Orleans,1989
Portland Chapter AIA Annual Convention, Portland, Oregon, 1989
Carnegie Mellon University, Pittsburgh, Pennsylvania, 1990
Seattle AIA Annual Convention at the University of Washington, 1990
Kanto Gakuin University, Yokohama/Tokyo, 1990
NEOCON, Chicago, 1990
Virginia State AIA Convention, Richmond, Virginia, 1991
Kansas City AIA, Kansas City, Missouri, 1991

Symposia

'New American Architecture' at Technical University, Helsinki, 1980
New Chicago Architecture', at Palazzo Della Gran Guardia, Verona, 1981
'New Directions in European Architecture', at University of Rome, 1984
'A Search for Meaning: Present Directions in Architecture', international symposium in honour of Christian Norberg-Schulz's 60-Year Anniversary, at Grand Hotel, Oslo, 1986

'The New Moderns', Royal Institute of British Architects, London, sponsored by the Academy Group and the Royal Academy of Arts, September, 1990
'Design Awards Symposium' of Los Angeles Chapter AIA, at Hollywood Building, Los Angeles, October, 1991
'Architecture in Arcadia', the Royal Academy of Arts, London, sponsored by the Academy Group and the Royal Academy of Arts, March, 1992
'Theory & Experimentation', the Royal Academy of Arts, London, sponsored by the Academy Group and the Royal Academy of Arts, June, 1992

Registrations and Affiliations
Registered Architect, States of Michigan, Washington, Wisconsin
Licensed Architect to practise in Norway/Sweden/Denmark
American Institute of Architects (National): AIA Member
New York Chapter, American Institute of Architects
Who's Who in America, 1986-1992
Norwegian Architects' Association: MNAL member

Selected Writings by Peter Pran
Peter Pran, Oswald Grube and Franz Schulze, 100 Years of Architecture in Chicago, Continuity of Structure and Form, Follet Publishing Co, Chicago, 1976.
'Recent Buildings by Mies van der Rohe', Byggekunst 48, No 7, 1966, pp 170-181, Norwegian Architecture Association, Oslo, (Scandinavian/Norwegian architectural magazine).
'A Study of Large Clear Span Structures', Column, No 34, 1970, pp 7-16, Yarvata Iron and Steel Co, Tokyo, Japan (editors: Art D'Acier Co).
'Plan for an Exhibition Hall with Suspended Roof', Bauen und Wohnen, No 8, 1970, pp 285-289, editors in Switzerland and West Germany (international architectural magazine).
'Large Clear Span Structures', Byggekunst 53, No 1, 1971, pp 4-8
'Urban Design', Journal for the College of Engineering, Washington State University, Pullman, Washington, 1972, co-authored with Dorman Anderson.
'The Completion of the Sears Office Building in Chicago', Verdens Gang, Oslo, No 9, 1973, pp 22-23, presentation and introduction by Jan Christensen.
'The Positive Use of Highrise Buildings', Inland Architect, 20, No 1, January, 1976, pp 15-16, AIA and IA, Chicago.
'Introduction to the Chicago Architecture Exhibition', co-authored with Franz Schulze, Inland Architect, 20, No 3, March, 1976, pp 10-14, AIA and IA, Chicago.
'Build Me A City', co-authored with Franz Schulze, Midwest Magazine – Chicago Sun Times, April 25, 1976, Chicago.
'The Diversity of Design among Chicago Architects Today', L'architettura, Rome, December, 1977, pp 434-474 (international architectural magazine, editor Bruno Zevi).
'Virginio Ferrari: A Leading Sculptor in Chicago', Cimaise, No 156-157, 1981, Paris (international art and architecture magazine).
'A New Modern Architecture', Architecture & Urbanism, January issue, 1985, Tokyo.
'Our Approach to Modern Architecture', Proa, architecture magazine #380, 1989, Bogota.
'Progressive Museum Architecture', statement in 'New Museology', Art & Design magazine, 7/8 1990, Academy Editions, London.
'The New Modern Architecture', in 'The New Modern Aesthetic', Architectural Design magazine, 7/8 1990, Academy Editions, London.
'Museum Architecture', Proa, architecture magazine, #407, 1991, Bogota, Columbia.
'A New Modern Architecture for the Third Millennium' in Architecture for the Third Millennium, eds M Fabbri, D Pastore, Fondazione Adriano Olivetti, Italy, 1991.

Recent Articles and Presentations on Peter Pran and Ellerbe Becket
Fazlur Kahn, 'The Future of High-Rise Structures' in Progressive Architecture, October 1972, pp 79-85, includes the presentation of a 100-storey highrise complex for Vancouver, designed under the direction of Professor Peter Pran, by James Meyer.
Colin Amery, 'The Most Architectural City', Architectural Review (Chicago issue), London, October 1977.
Paul Gapp, 'Townhouse Design Exhibit', Chicago Tribune, June 4, 178, Chicago, Illinois, USA, includes presentation of Peter Pran's first prize-winning Townhouse.
Paul Goldberger, 'Where is Architecture Headed?', The New York Times Magazine, October 18, 1987.
Carter Horsley, 'The Best New York Buildings of the Year', New York Post, December 29, 1988, includes JFK Terminal by Peter Pran of Ellerbe Becket.
Christian Norberg-Schulz, 'Peter Pran in New York', Arkitektnytt, April, 1983, Oslo.
Bruno Zevi, 'La Scuola di Enna', L'Espresso, March 20, 1988, pp 177-178, Rome and Milan, Italy, review of the exhibit 'New York Architects' in Enna, Sicily including the work of Peter Pran and Carlos Zapata of Ellerbe Becket.
Karen Stein, 'Against All Odds', feature article on the recent design work of Peter Pran and Carlos Zapata of Ellerbe Becket, New York Architectural Record, April 1989, New York.
Joseph Giovannini, Introduction to New York Architecture #2, 1989, NYC/AIA Design Awards, AIA, discussion of Peter Pran's design awards.
Lars Elton, 'The Prize Winner Peter Pran' in Aftenposten, Oslo, March 3, 1989.
Douglas Davis, 'South Ferry Plaza in Manhattan by Peter Pran & Carlos Zapata', in 10 on 10: The Critics' Choice, NYC/AIA, 1989.
Flemming Frost and Helle Juul, 'New Terminal at JFK' by Peter Pran & Carlos Zapata of Ellerbe Becket, Skala, #17/18, 1989, Copenhagen.
Thomas Fisher: 'Communicating Ideas Artfully', (includes JFK Terminal), Progressive Architecture, June 1989.
Marcello Fabbri: 'University of Minnesota, School of Architecture, by Peter Pran, Design Principal, Ellerbe Becket, New York', Controspazio, May-June, 1990, Milan, Italy.
Kenneth Frampton, 'New York's Narcosis: Reflections from an Archimedean Point', New York Architecture 1970-1990, Prestel, Munich and Rizzoli, New York, 1990, pp 46-50 includes an evaluation of Peter Pran's recent work.
Douglas Davis, 'New York in the Next Century', New York Architecture 1970-1990, Prestel, Munich and Rizzoli, New York, 1990, pp 51-53, includes an evaluation of Peter Pran's recent work.
Clifford A Pearson, 'Modernism in Motion' 'New executive offices by Peter Pran and Carlos Zapata put an accounting firm on the cutting edge', 'Deloitte & Touche Headquarters by Ellerbe Becket, Architects', Architectural Record, May, 1990, New York.
Ulf Grönvold, 'Pran in New York', feature article on Peter Pran's recent work at Ellerbe Becket, New York, Byggekunst #5-6, 1990, Oslo.
Thomas Fisher, 'Ellerbe Becket explores from coast to coast Modernism's Leading Edge', Progressive Architecture, October 1991.
Hiroko Sueyoshi, 'Deloitte & Touche, by Ellerbe Becket with Peter Pran & Carlos Zapata', World Space Design, Vol II, 1991, Tokyo.
Editorial article, 'Deloitte & Touche, Ellerbe Beckett, Peter Pran & Carlos Zapata', Crée, Architecture Interieure, June, 1991, Paris.
M Fabbri and D Pastore, 'Recent Designs by Peter Pran of Ellerbe Becket', Architecture for the Third Millennium, Olivetti Foundation,

Italy, 1991.
Amalia de Vargas Rubiano, 'Peter Pran & Carlos Zapata of Ellerbe Becket, New York: Recent Work', Proa International, *#407, November, 1991, Bogota.*
Joan Oakman, 'Introduction' to the 1991 NYC/AIA Design Awards, New York Architecture, *Volume 4.*
Contemporary Architectural Drawings of Avery Library and Art Collection, ed Janet Parks, Columbia University, 1991, Pomegranate, San Francisco.
Ulf Grönvold, 'Peter Pran Wins Three Competitions', Arkitektnytt #7, 1992, Oslo.
Graham Vickers, 'Wild Entry', feature article on the new Academic Building at the State University of New York, Binghamton, New York, with Peter Pran, Design Principal of Ellerbe Becket, World Architecture *#2, Spring 1992, London.*
Theory and Experimentation, ed Andreas Papadakis, presents work by 20 architects and includes recent work by Peter Pran of Ellerbe Becket, Academy Editions, London, 1992.

TV Programme
Jahn Otto Johansen presented a 30-minute feature programme 'Peter Pran and his Building Designs in New York', on main Norwegian TV, December 5, 1986.

Further Work Published in Books and Journals
John Winter, Industrial Architecture, *Studio Vista, London, 1970.*
Oswald Crube, Industrial Buildings and Factories, *Praeger, New York, 1972.*
'An Exhibition Hall for Chicago', Bauen und Wohnen *No 8, 1970, pp 285-289 (Editors in Germany and Switzerland).*
John Hix, Glasshouses, *Pall Mall Press, London, 1977.*
'Summer House, Ula Norway, by Peter Pran', Byggekunst *#5, 1978, Norwegian Architecture Association, Oslo.*
'Peter Pran's design of Facilities Center, Indianapolis', Progressive Architecture, *June 1980; part of an article on new Chicago architecture, by Nory Miller, p 79.*
Alfred Swenson and Pao Chi Chang, Architectural Education at Illinois Institute of Technology, IIT, Chicago, 1980. *Presentation of Exhibition Hall for Chicago by Peter Pran in collaboration with Myron Goldsmith, Fazlur Khan and David Sharpe.*
Creation and Recreation: America Draws, ed Juhanni Pallasmaa, Museum of Finnish Architecture, Helsinki, 1980.
Vincenzo Pavan and Maurizio Casari, New Chicago Architecture, *Rizzoli International, New York, 1981.*
'Family Health Center, Gary, Indiana', Architectural Record, *August 1981.*
'IIT Townhouses and Parking Facility in Chicago by Peter Pran', Bauen und Wohnen, *May, 1981 (ed Jean-Claude Steinegger, Zurich).*
Werner Blaser, After Mies, The Continuation of the Chicago School of Architecture, *Van Nostrand, New York and London, 1982.*
'Facilities Center, Indianapolis by Peter Pran', Domus, *May, 1983, Milan.*
Heinrich Klotz, The Revision of Modernism, *Deutsches Architekturmuseum and Prestel, Munich, 1985.*
Douglas Davis, Modern Redux, *New York University, New York, 1986.*
In Architettura *#13, April 1987, Palermo and Medina, presentation of 'New York Architects', exhibit in Italy.*
G Guerrera, New York Architects, *with introductions by Kenneth Frampton and Livio Dimitriu, Edizioni Medina, Italy, 1988.*
Douglas Davis, 'The End of Style', Art in America, *June, 1987.*
New York Architecture *#1, NYC/AIA Design Awards issue, NYC/AIA, 1988.*
'Peter Pran of Ellerbe Becket in New York', BAF-News of Bergen Architect's Association, No 3, 1989, Bergen, Norway. Presentation of JFK and Schibsted projects (Ed NR Övsthus).
'Recent Buildings and Projects by Peter Pran and Carlos Zapata', Proa International *#380, 1989, Bogota, Columbia.*
New York Architecture *#2, NYC/AIA Design Awards issue, NYC/AIA, 1989.*
New York Architecture *#3, NYC/AIA Design Awards issue, NYC/AIA, 1990.*
Heinrich Klotz and Luminita Saban, New York Architecture 1970-1990, *Prestel, Munich & Rizzoli, New York (Reprinted also with Taipai Fine Arts Museum for a special Taiwan issue in 1991).*
'New Building Designs by Peter Pran & Carlos Zapata of Ellerbe Becket', Proa International *#407, 1991, Bogota, Columbia.*
New York Architecture *#4, NYC/AIA Design Awards issue, NYC/AIA, 1991.*
'The New Modern Aesthetic', Architectural Design, *7/8 1990, Academy Editions, London, designs by Peter Pran and Carlos Zapata of Ellerbe Becket.*

ELLERBE BECKET
Architects and Engineers

John Gaunt, President and CEO
Robert Degenhardt, COO

Office Directors:
Jack Hunter, CCI, Minneapolis & CCI, New York
Jim Jenkins, Medical, Minneapolis
Rick Lincicome, Washington DC and New York
Ron Turner, Kansas City
Greg Nook, Los Angeles
Brad Hornburg, Construction Services, Minneapolis

Operations Directors:
Robert DeBruin, CCI, Minneapolis & CCI, New York
Barry Graham, Medical, Minneapolis
Randy Wood, Washington DC and New York
Paul Jorgensen, Kansas City
Bill Nara, Los Angeles
David Whitehouse, Construction Services, Minneapolis

Design Principals:
Richard Varda, CCI, Minneapolis
Peter Pran, CCI, New York
Frank Nemeth, Medical, Minneapolis
John Waugh, Medical, Minneapolis
Mike Jones, Washington DC
Mehrdad Yazdani, Los Angeles
Bill Johnson, Kansas City

Ellerbe Becket, the largest architecture-engineering firm in the USA, with a staff of 1000 persons, has offices in Los Angeles, Minneapolis, Kansas City, Washington DC, New York and Tokyo.